Lecture Notes in Economics and Mathematical Systems

526

Springer
Berlin
Heidelberg
New York
Hong Kong
London
Milan
Paris
Tokyo

Carlos F. Daganzo

A Theory
of Supply Chains

 Springer

Author

Prof. Carlos F. Daganzo
University of California
416 McLaughlin Hall
Berkeley, CA 94707
USA

Cataloging-in-Publication Data applied for

A catalog record for this book is available from the Library of Congress.

Bibliographic information published by Die Deutsche Bibliothek
Die Deutsche Bibliothek lists this publication in the Deutsche Nationalbibliografie;
detailed bibliographic data is available in the Internet at <http://dnb.ddb.de>.

ISSN 0075-8450
ISBN 3-540-00288-X Springer-Verlag Berlin Heidelberg New York

Springer-Verlag Berlin Heidelberg New York
a part of Springer Science+Business Media

http://www.springer.de

© Springer-Verlag Berlin Heidelberg 2003 / Carlos F. Daganzo
Printed in Germany

Typesetting: Camera ready by author
Cover design: *Erich Kirchner*, Heidelberg

Printed on acid-free paper   SPIN: 10989722   55/3111   5 4 3 2 1

Preface

This work was stimulated by a comment made by a former student (Prof. Alan Erera of Georgia Tech) in connection with an inventory stability game he was going to play in one of his logistics classes. This was the well-known "beer-game" that is often played in business schools to illustrate the "bullwhip" effect in supply chains. Al had said to me that he did not have to tell his students how to reorder replacement parts from the other members of the supply chain because he knew from experience that the order sizes the players would generate as the game progressed would become chaotic anyhow. Since I had not played the beer game, his assertion was intriguing to me. Why would such an unstructured game always lead to the same undesirable effect? Did it have something to do with psychology? What is it that players did to generate instabilities? I posed these questions to other people but could not get completely satisfactory answers. Thus, the bullwhip mystery remained, at least in my mind.

Since inventory chains are "conservative" systems analogous to a traffic stream, and since traffic flow models exhibit similar effects (the instability of automobile platoons and of certain numerical methods being two notable examples) I suspected that traffic flow theory might shed some light on the puzzle. This possibility became very intriguing to me because it meant that efforts to solve the puzzle might unify two research areas dear to my heart, "logistics" and "traffic flow". At the very least, they could show a strong connection between the two.

After several months of study, the results by mid 2001 were encouraging. Not only there seemed to be a strong connection between "logistics" and "traffic flow", but it appeared that "queuing theory" was a third leg of the stool too. In addition, three main findings stood out: (i) the apparent cause of the bullwhip effect; (ii) an efficient way to stabilize supply chains without centralized control; and (iii) a way to choose an optimum control policy subject to stability constraints. These ideas formed the basis for an extended "theory of supply chains." Because the results were obtained with methods rarely used in inventory analysis they had to be presented in an unconventional way, requiring new notation and terminology. Therefore, I needed feedback to figure out how best to proceed.

I gave a series of four lectures at U.C. Berkeley in the fall of 2001. They were attended by three colleagues (professors Mike Cassidy, Phil Kaminsky and Samer Madanat from the CEE and IEOR departments) and by 12 of our most advanced PhD students. The comments of this select audience helped me refine the rough lecture notes into something resembling a monograph. They convinced me that a comprehensive, self-contained document would be the best publication venue for the complete work, and that one or two journal articles could then be used to summarize the main results. This monograph is the self-contained document.

Phil Kaminsky and (PhD candidate) Alejandro Lago offered valuable comments on preliminary versions. A brief paper summarizing the first half of the monograph was also circulated to key colleagues, and its highlights were presented at a few universities (U. Dresden, Georgia Tech, U. Montreal, and U.C. Berkeley (twice)). The comments of everyone who helped me are gratefully acknowledged. The perspective of professors Anton Kleywegt (Georgia Tech) and Paul Zipkin (Duke University) was particularly helpful. I also wish to thank PhD students Anne Goodchild, Jorge Laval, Juan Carlos Muñoz, Yuwei Li and Yanfeng Ouyang for drawing most of the figures and helping put the manuscript in its final form. The work was partly supported by grants from the University of California Transportation Center.

I should finally note that these lecture notes have not been used in the classroom in their final form. Therefore, they may contain errors; hopefully not too many. It goes without saying that all errors are exclusively mine. When found, they will be posted on the publications section of my web page: http://www.ce.berkeley.edu/~daganzo/.

Carlos Daganzo
Berkeley
November 8, 2002

Table of Contents

1. Introduction

1.1 The problem

A supply chain is a network of suppliers that produce goods, both, for one another and for generic customers. Goods travel from origin-suppliers to destination-customers, possibly visiting intermediate suppliers and being altered or recombined in the process. Conservation rules at each supplier, define its outputs as a function of its inputs. The rates at which goods of different types flow over this network depend on the customer demand, the flow of information (orders) across suppliers, and on the algorithms/policies that the suppliers use to place orders and replenish their inventories.[1]

For the most part, these notes examine the operation of a serial supply chain with a unique item type, where each supplier j receives all its goods from $j+1$ and ships them to $j-1$. In the inventory control literature such a system would be called a "multi-echelon", (or multi-stage) serial system. See Peterson and Silver (1979) and Zipkin (2000) for inventory management treatises. Extensions to general multi-commodity networks are presented in the last chapter.

Of special interest are supply chains where the reorder policies are exclusively based on local information; i.e., where the decisions of supplier j are based on its own status and the order history of $j-1$. These chains are here said to be "autonomous." The instability of autonomous chains is a well-known phenomenon. By instability, it is meant the increased variability in the order sizes and the inventory levels experienced with the suppliers as j increases. The name "bullwhip effect" has been coined to describe it—perhaps because the suppliers farthest away from the customers feel as

---

[1] The word "policy" is often used in the inventory control literature to denote simple re-order rules. Because in these notes the re-order rules can be as complicated as desired, allowing for any degree of adaptation to varying demand conditions, the word "algorithm" is often used. The words algorithm, policy and rule will be used interchangeably.

if they were at the end of a bullwhip.[2] A "beer game" is even used in business schools to illustrate it; see Sterman (1989), or Goodwin and Franklin (1994) for a detailed discussion. The bullwhip effect is so prevalent that the aforementioned beer-game does not have to be structured very carefully, and it invariably leads to instabilities (Erera, 2001).

Despite its importance, our understanding of the bullwhip effect is still incomplete. Although, there has been some limited succes in analyzing the phenomenon and identifying some of its causes for special cases,[3] a general theory of supply chains with arbitrary demand inputs and replenishment algorithms has not yet been put forward. These lecture notes attempt to fill this gap. They add to current knowledge by presenting a systematic analysis of all possible algorithms under general demand conditions— stochastic or deterministic; time-dependent or stationary; ergodic or not. Therefore, in these notes stability is an intrinsic property of an algorithm, independent of the demand. This goal requires that stability be defined differently than by the behavior of a "variance". As in control theory (see e.g., Stengel, 1994) two definitions are used. We call them: "*stability in the small*" and "*stability in the large*". Stability in the small means that any infinitesimal perturbation in the customer demand input when the system is in a steady state generates order size and inventory perturbations that are also infinitesimal, even as $j \to \infty$. This must be true for all possible steady states and perturbation types. Stability in the large means that the order sizes and the inventories must be bounded across all j and all times, *for any imaginable realization of the demand process*. (Clearly, stability in the large implies that the variance of the inventory at j for an ergodic demand process is bounded across j.)   A policy that is both, stable in the small and in the large will be said to be "*strongly stable*".

These notes develop necessary and sufficient conditions to establish whether arbitrary algorithms are stable in the small. It is shown that to re-

---

[2] Forrester (1961) is usually cited as the first academic reference that explicitly describes the phenomenon. Additional discussion and anecdotal evidence can be found in Magee and Boodman (1967), Buffa and Miller (1979), Blackburn (1991), Lee et al (1997a) and Simchi-Levi et al. (2000), among others.

[3] Metters (1996) quantifies costs for various demand assumptions under optimal finite-horizon replenishment policy. Lee at al (1997b), Ryan (1997) and Chen et al (2000) show that order variance increase with supplier level in periodic review algorithms with stationary demand. Graves (1999) analyzes base-stock policies with special cases of non-stationary demand. Related work can also be found in the economics literature, by Holt et al (1960), Blinder (1986), Kahn (1987), Ramey (1991) and Naish (1994) among others. Most of this work uses stylized inventory models to explain at the macroeconomic level the causes that make production more variable than sales, as observed empirically.

duce inventories during periods of low demand, autonomous policies must use future order commitments if they are to be stable.[4] A dual relationship between autonomous supply chains and serial queues is shown to exist. Thus, general results for the stability of queuing networks are obtained as a byproduct. These results are also presented.

The notes also introduce a class of strongly stable, commitment-based algorithms that allow suppliers to maintain inventories close to any demand-dependent target of their choice. With algorithms in this class, suppliers can act in their own self-interest, without the bullwhip effect. When suppliers do this (minimize their own costs without regard to others) we say that they act "user-optimally". The notes then show how to find a stable, user-optimal rule. It is found that the total system cost obtained with user-optimal rules is close to the globally optimum cost with coordinated procedures. This is called the "system-optimum" cost.

Mathematical procedures from the field of traffic flow theory are used, with modifications. The techniques are successful because a supply chain is somewhat analogous to a freeway, where the items are cars, and the suppliers, freeway detectors. Modifications are needed because the rules of motion (i.e. the management algorithms) in the supply chain management problem are not given. This introduces additional degrees of freedom into the problem, including an optimization angle. In any case, by looking at the supply chain problem in this way, a potentially useful connection between two separate fields of study is unveiled.

The lecture notes are organized as follows. The rest of this chapter introduces basic terminology and ways of displaying data. Chapters 2 and 3 focus on algorithms; Chap. 2 classifies them, and Chap. 3 discusses their basic properties. Chapter 4 develops stability tests for homogeneous chains, where all suppliers use the same policy, and discusses their implications. This chapter also presents the duality results for queuing systems. Chapter 5 shows how strongly stable policies can be constructed. Section 5.1 defines a family of strongly stable "targets" for algorithms to track. These results are used in Section 5.2 to develop a family of strongly stable policies that can track these targets. The family includes "just-in-time" policies as a special case. Chapter 6 shows how to estimate total cost with both, autonomous user-optimal, and coordinated system-optimal opera-

---

[4] The convenience of advanced demand information has been analyzed for single-stage production systems in some special cases; see Hariharan and Zipkin (1995), Gallego and Ozer (2001) and, Karesman et al (2002), among others. In the case of supply chains, Naish (1994) and Graves (1999) acknowledge that the bullwhip effect is always present in the absence of reliable future demand information, but their conclusions are based only on particular inventory and demand models.

tions. It is shown that user-optimal operation is asymptotically optimal if the demand varies slowly. Chapter 7 concludes these notes with extensions of the results to non-linear, multi-commodity, multi-destination networks.

1.2 Terminology and data representation

A serial supply chain is shown in Fig. 1.1a, where j ($j = 0, 1, 2, \dots J$) is the supplier index, and arrows denote the flow of information and physical items. The figure shows that when an order is placed an acknowledgment is sent in return and, some time later, the physical items follow the acknowledgement. At any given point in time and for every supplier, there is a physical inventory of items, a virtual inventory of order acknowledgements, a number of items in transit to and from the supplier, and a set of orders that have been placed but not yet fulfilled. Obviously, much data is relevant to the performance of the system, and keeping track of it all can be complicated. This section describes a way in which all this information can be organized to facilitate an analysis.

It is customary in the production-inventory literature to consider the history of orders, production and delivery batches and inventory levels as the primary system descriptors. These variables are also fundamental here, but we will find it convenient to keep track of them with curves of cumulative flow, as is conventional in some engineering fields. No generality is lost by this approach. Cumulative plots are useful tools when one must analyze the flow of items past one or several restrictions. They have been used in engineering for a long time. For example, their usefulness in hydrologic synthesis has been recognized for over a century. (In this field they form the basis of a technique known as "mass curve analysis" for determining the capacity of reservoirs; Linsley and Franzini, 1955.) They were first used in traffic engineering in the 1950's (Moskowitz, 1954), rediscovered in the 1960's (Gazis and Potts, 1965) and introduced to queuing theory at about the same time (see e.g., Newell, 1971). It was Gordon Newell, though, who demonstrated their full potential as an analysis tool by showing how the kinematic waves of traffic flow theory could be tracked in space-time in a very simple way using cumulative plots (Newell, 1993). This beautiful paper unified queuing theory and traffic flow theory in a remarkable way. It is because of Newell's influence in these two fields that the cumulative curves used in these notes shall be called "Newell curves."

Newell curves, $N_j(t)$, are curves of cumulative count (integrals of the flow) at different locations, j, with integration constants such that vertical

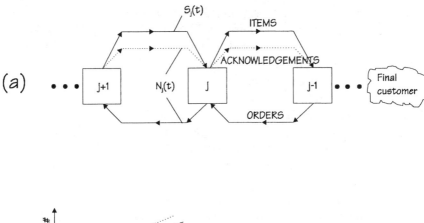

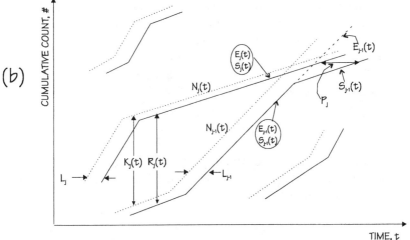

Figure 1.1. Flows on a supply chain: (a) Physical diagram; (b) N-curve representation.

separations between curves represent accumulations between locations. For unidirectional flow the curves are non-decreasing. With discrete items, such as cars or most goods, they increase in jumps as step functions. With fluids conveyed on pipes they increase continuously. The horizontal separation between two curves for a specific item number is the time between the instants at which the specific item number was reached at the two locations. For FIFO (first-in-first-out) systems this is the trip time of the item in question between the two locations. When there is a minimum trip time, M, between locations j and $j-1$, the two N-curves must be horizontally separated by at least M time units at all ordinates. Since the N-curves are non-decreasing this can be expressed by the inequality: $N_j(t) \geq N_{j-1}(t-M)$.

In our case, three sets of curves will be used: $\{N_j\}$, $\{E_j\}$ and $\{S_j\}$. The first set tracks the orders placed by each supplier j. The second set tracks expectations, i.e., the physical items that should have arrived at j based on its orders (assuming no glitches), and the third set tracks actual deliveries. By assuming that the N-curves are monotonic, we are implicitly assuming that order cancellations are not allowed.[5]

To interpret the first set, we imagine the following. When an order is placed by j (from $j+1$), an acknowledgement is immediately sent from $j+1$ to j, as suggested by the dotted arrows on Fig. 1.1a. The acknowledgement includes the highest item number (#) that will be sent when the order is filled a lead-time later. Note that # is increased by the order size with every request. Curves of this set, $N_j(t)$, give the acknowledgement number received at time t by supplier j. This is also the order number received at t by supplier $j + 1$. Therefore, the difference between the number of the last order placed by j (from $j+1$), $N_j(t)$, and the last order received by j (from $j-1$), $N_{j-1}(t)$, is the inventory of order acknowledgements (orders placed minus orders received) at j:

$$K_j(t) = N_j(t) - N_{j-1}(t). \tag{1.1}$$

Although $K_j(t)$ should be positive in most cases, nothing physical prevents this variable from taking on negative values. This could happen for example if, due to a computer glitch, supplier j were to stop placing orders. The order acknowledgement curves, N_j, are the dotted lines in Fig. 1.1b. (To simplify the figure, the discrete steps corresponding to specific orders have been smoothed out, as if the item flow was continuous, but nothing said in this section requires continuity.) The horizontal separation between the curves is the lag in the order number processed at consecutive suppliers; i.e. the "acknowledgement trip time".

The physical arrivals expected at j are related to its orders by

$$N_j(t) = E_j(t+L_j), \tag{1.2}$$

where $E_j(t)$ is the cumulative item number expected at j by time t and $L_j \geq 0$ is a deterministic lead-time. The lead-time is calculated on the assumption that supplier $j+1$ does not stock out and can serve all the demand without delay. If supplier $j+1$ holds inventories of finished products and ships items as soon as they are ordered, then L_j equals the transportation

---

[5] This assumption will be dropped later on.

time. If the supplier holds inventories of unfinished products, and makes them to order, then L_j equals the sum of the in-house production/handling time and the transportation time; this will be called the "processing" time for $j+1$, P_{j+1}. Our discussion applies to both forms of operation and to mixed forms. We will soon see that it also holds for non-deterministic relations between N and E. In the deterministic case, the E-curves are just horizontal translations of the N-curves; see the solid lines of Fig. 1.1b.

The third set of curves, $S_j(t)$ pertain to the actual arrival of physical items at j. (Note that we assume that all demand is always fulfilled with or without delays, i.e., backlogging is allowed). If items are not delayed the S-curves coincide with the E-curves, and this occurs for the most part on Fig. 1.1b. The general rule for delays is that a specific item, #, should arrive at j at the later of two times: (i) its expected arrival time (if $j+1$ has enough stock on hand when the order was placed), or else (ii) the time when the item arrives at supplier $j+1$ plus the processing time for $j+1$ (the sum of the transportation and in-house production/handling times). Therefore, for a supply chain with customer $j = 0$ and suppliers $j = 1, 2, \ldots J$, the S-curves and the E-curves are related by

$$S_{j-1}(t) = min\{E_{j-1}(t),\ S_j(t-P_j)\} \qquad \text{for } j = 1, 2, \ldots J \qquad (1.3a)$$

and

$$S_J(t) = E_J(t). \qquad (1.3b)$$

In other words, the arrival curve at j-1 is just the lower envelope of the expectation curve for j-1 and the shifted arrival curve for j. When the envelope matches the former, the supply chain is operating as expected. When it matches the latter, demand is backlogged and items arrive with a delay. The top right part of Fig. 1.1b shows how delays arise when expectations (dashed line) run ahead of possible arrivals (solid line), and the two curves diverge. The number of items delayed at time t is $E_{j-1}(t) - S_{j-1}(t)$; i.e. the vertical separation between the expectation and the actual arrival curves. This is also the number of orders not shipped on time by supplier j; i.e., its order backlog. The item inventory of supplier j at time t (including items in transit to $j-1$), $R_j(t)$, is given by the vertical separation between the S_j and S_{j-1} curves (see Fig. 1.1b):

$$R_j(t) = S_j(t)\ -\ S_{j-1}(t). \qquad (1.4)$$

We are interested in these notes in the behavior of reliable supply chains, where back-orders are rare. It turns out that such a condition can be expressed in terms of the order curves alone. We have just seen that a condition for no backorders at all is $E_{j-1}(t) \leq S_j(t-P_j)$ for all t and j. However, since $E_{j-1}(t) = N_{j-1}(t-L_{j-1})$ by virtue of (1.2), and $S_j(t-P_j) \leq E_j(t-P_j)$ by virtue of (1.3a), the no-backorder condition can be written as $N_{j-1}(t-L_{j-1}) \leq E_j(t-P_j)$. Since $E_j(t-P_j) = N_j(t-P_j-L_j)$, again by virtue of (1.2), an equivalent inequality is terms of the N-curves alone is $N_{j-1}(t-L_{j-1}) \leq N_j(t-P_j-L_j)$. This can be written more succinctly as follows:

$$N_{j-1}(t+M_j) \leq N_j(t), \qquad \text{(reliability condition)} \qquad (1.5)$$

where $M_j = P_j + L_j - L_{j-1}$.

Equation (1.5) guarantees on-time deliveries and prevents stock-outs. The equation says that, for perfect reliability, the lag between the order times at consecutive suppliers for a specific item must exceed a constant, M_j. This "minimum order lag" equals the "processing time" if $L_j = L_{j-1}$; e.g., if the chain is homogeneous. If equation (1.5) holds most of the time, and is only violated slightly when it does not hold, then the backorder episodes should be infrequent and small. It is in this approximate sense that (1.5) will be used as a constraint in these notes. Note that equation (1.5) can also be justified for systems with random processing times. In this case, M_j is simply a sufficiently large order-lag that would guarantee on-time deliveries *most* of the time.

Finally, note from (1.2) and (1.3) that if one is given a set of N-curves, then the E- and S-curves are uniquely determined. This means that the N-curves embody all the relevant information of our problem. Thus, a complete theory of supply chains can be formulated in terms of the N-curves alone. The following chapter explains this in more detail and examines the possible kinds of reorder strategies that can be used to determine the N-curves.

2. Algorithms / Policies

An algorithm (or "policy") is a rule that suppliers follow to generate orders. The output of these policies is a set of N-curves driven by the customer demands, $N_0(t)$. Policies that always yield non-negative orders (i.e., allow no cancellations) produce non-decreasing N-curves. They will be said to be "monotone". Monotonicity is a desirable property in practical applications, and will be required of the algorithms developed in Chapter 5. We have already seen that monotonic algorithms avoid backorders (approximately) if (1.5) is satisfied (approximately) for all possible customer demands. This reliability condition will also be demanded of the proposed algorithms. The analysis of the bullwhip effect done in Chapter 4 is completely general, however. It applies to non-monotone and unreliable policies.

In these notes we will focus on discrete-time algorithms where the $N(t)$ are step functions with jumps on a time lattice, $t_n = nh$, and we will write $N_{j,n}$ for $N_j(t_n)$. Here n is an integer and h is the lattice interval. No generality is lost by the chosen focus, since by letting h tend to zero the results can be extended to continuous time.

2.1 The canonical form: order-based and inventory-based policies

Given the customer demands and an initial set of order numbers $\{N_{j,0}\}$, or another suitable set of initial conditions, the supplier reorder algorithms must provide the jumps in the N-curves for $t_n \geq t_0$; i.e., the order sizes, $Q_{j,n} = N_{j,n+1} - N_{j,n}$. This, however, can be done in many ways, depending on the data that are used to determine the orders.

In the most complicated case, corresponding to a coordinated supply chain with information shared across all suppliers, $Q_{j,n}$ would be determined from all past information prior to $t = t_n$. We argued in Chapter 1, however, that E- and S-curves could be determined from the N-curves if the lead- and processing times were deterministic. Therefore, all the relevant information for decision-making is embodied in the N-curves, and we can assume without loss of generality that $Q_{j,n}$ is exclusively determined from the history of the N-curves. This is also reasonable for systems with random lead- and processing times if the chain is operated reliably. The causal structure of these kinds of chains is displayed in Fig. 2.1a. Solid dots and solid lines represent the data used to determine the order placed at the point highlighted by a square.

For autonomous policies, supplier j could use the history of N_{j-1}, and perhaps its own. However, its own order history is redundant information since it can be constructed from the history of N_{j-1} and the initial conditions ($N_{j,0}$ and $N_{j-1,0}$) by applying the algorithm. It should, thus, be clear that only the history of N_{j-1} and the $N_{j,0}$ value--or the value of N_j at any other point in time--are needed to express a general autonomous rule. We will use $N_{j,n}$ as the value for supplier j. Figure 2.1b displays the causal structure of the general autonomous policy, using this convention.

It is also possible to define semi-autonomous policies where suppliers collaborate in small groups. Figure 2.1c depicts the causal structure of a policy involving two levels of the chain.

Note too that for serial queuing systems in which customers flow in the direction of decreasing server number j (as in the supply chain) the departure rate from server j-1 is determined by the queue length, and (possibly) by the history of arrivals and departures. Thus, queuing systems have the causal structure of Fig. 2.1d; i.e., a mirror image of the autonomous supply chain. We will see in Chap. 4 that this symmetry is at the heart of the duality results between queues and inventory systems.

Returning now to autonomous policies for supply chain problems, we see from Fig. 2.1b that the value of N_j at time n+1 can only be a function of $N_{j,n}$, $N_{j-1,n}$, $N_{j-1,n-1}$, $N_{j-1,n-2}$... We will restrict our attention in these notes to policies were this argument list is finite, stretching back in time for a maximum of B periods.[1] This is reasonable on practical grounds.[2] Any such expression can always be put in the following "canonical form":

$$N_{j,n+1} = N_{j-1,n} + F_j(N_{j,n}, N_{j-1,n}, N_{j-1,n-1}, N_{j-1,n-2}... N_{j-1,n-B}) .\qquad(2.1)$$

---

[1] The list of arguments is allowed to be shorter when the process begins, if there is no sufficient history.

[2] Since practical policies should try to dissipate the effects of transient phenomena, the effects of transient events in the distant past should have little impact on order rates. Thus, it makes sense to limit the list of arguments as suggested.

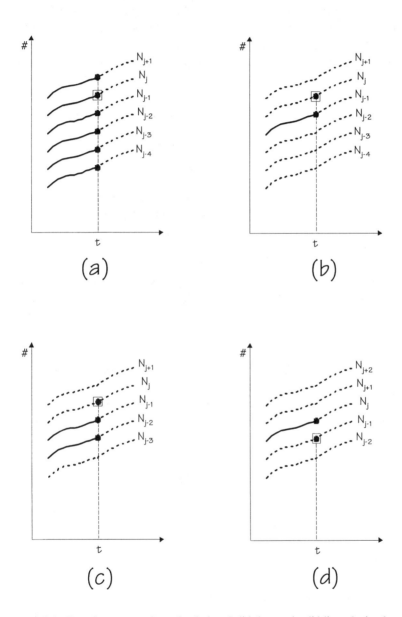

Figure 2.1. Causal structure of supply chains. Solid dots and solid lines depict data used to determine the jump of the *N*-curve at the point highlighted by a square in four cases: (a) general, non-anticipative; (b) autonomous, pull, non-anticipative; (c) 2-level, pull, non-anticipative; (d) autonomous, push, non-anticipative.

Note that $N_{j-1,n}$ is the cumulative number of orders received by j immediately before placing an order, and $N_{j,n+1}$ is the cumulative number that will be reached after the order. Thus, "F_j" simply expresses the desired "order inventory position" immediately after orders are placed. It will be called the *kernel* of the policy. The order quantity is obtained by subtracting $N_{j,n}$ from both sides of (2.1). It will sometimes be convenient to write it as:

$$Q_{j,n+1} = Y_j(N_{j,n}, N_{j-1,n}, N_{j-1,n-1}, N_{j-1,n-2} \cdots N_{j-1,n-B}) \,. \tag{2.2}$$

Since the order-history of supplier $j-1$ up to time n is always known to j, this supplier can iterate (2.1) for increasing n to obtain its own sequence of N-values. This is true for all j.

For a kernel F_j to be "proper", its output should be independent of the origin of coordinates used to label the order numbers. In other words, if one adds or subtracts a constant from all the arguments of the kernel, the order inventory position should remain unchanged. This implies that the sum of the partial derivatives of a differentiable kernel should be 1. Therefore, we can subtract $N_{j-1,n}$ from all the arguments in (2.1) to express the policy. The result is that the (new) order inventory position is a function of the (current) order inventory, $K_{j,n}$, and a series of differences involving the N-values for $j-1$:

$$N_{j,n+1}-N_{j-1,n}=F_j(K_{j,n}, 0, N_{j-1,n-1} - N_{j-1,n}, N_{j-1,n-2} - N_{j-1,n}, \ldots, N_{j-1,n-B}-N_{j-1,n}).$$

Since these differences are sums of orders of $j-1$, this relation can also be expressed as a function of the current inventory and the order history of $j-1$, i.e.:

$$N_{j,n+1} - N_{j-1,n} = H_j(K_{j,n}, Q_{j-1,n-1}, Q_{j-1,n-2}, \ldots, Q_{j-1, n-B}).$$

And since the inventory order position is $N_{j,n+1} - N_{j-1,n} = N_{j,n+1} - N_{j,n} + N_{j,n} - N_{j-1,n} = Q_{j,n} + K_{j,n}$, we can also write:

$$Q_{j,n} = H_j(K_{j,n}, Q_{j-1,n-1}, Q_{j-1,n-2}, \ldots, Q_{j-1, n-B}) - K_{j,n} \,. \tag{2.3a}$$

This expression cannot be iterated, unless one has a way of updating the inventory inputs. However, the order inventory at time $n+1$ is just the inventory position, minus the orders to be received, i.e.:

$$K_{j,n+1} = H_j(K_{j,n}, Q_{j-1,n-1}, Q_{j-1,n-2}, \ldots, Q_{j-1, n-B}) - Q_{j-1,n} \,. \tag{2.3b}$$

Equations (2.3) can be iterated. They will be called the *order-inventory canonical form*. The function H_j will be called the *order-inventory kernel* or the *H-kernel*. If a policy is proper, it must admit an order-inventory canonical form with some kernel H_j. The equations are equivalent to (2.1). The only difference between (2.1) and (2.3) is that the two kernels F and H are expressed as functions of different arguments. Although (2.1) is simpler, (2.3) is more "conventional".

It should be noted that policies could also be expressed in non-canonical ways by manipulating equations (2.3). For example, we can take the first difference of (2.3a) with respect to n and write:

$$Q_{j,n} - Q_{j,n-1} = H_j(K_{j,n}, Q_{j-1,n-1}, Q_{j-1,n-2}, \dots, Q_{j-1, n-B}) -$$

$$H_j(K_{j,n-1}, Q_{j-1,n-2}, Q_{j-1,n-3}, \dots, Q_{j-1, n-B-1}) - (K_{j,n} - K_{j,n-1}).$$

Since inventories and orders are related by the conservation equation, $K_{j,n} = K_{j,n-1} + (Q_{j,n-1} - Q_{j-1,n-1})$, or $K_{j,n} - K_{j,n-1} = Q_{j,n-1} - Q_{j-1,n-1}$, we can substitute $(Q_{j,n-1} - Q_{j-1,n-1})$ for $(K_{j,n} - K_{j,n-1})$ in the above expression, eliminating $K_{j,n-1}$ from the list of inputs. Thus, $Q_{j,n}$ can be expressed exclusively as a function of $K_{j,n}$ and the order history of $j-1$, including $Q_{j-1, n-B-1}$; i.e.:

$$Q_{j,n} = H_j(K_{j,n}, Q_{j-1,n-1}, Q_{j-1,n-2}, \dots, Q_{j-1, n-B}) -$$

$$H_j(K_{j,n}+Q_{j-1,n-1}-Q_{j,n-1}, Q_{j-1,n-2}, Q_{j-1,n-3}, \dots, Q_{j-1,n-B-1}) + Q_{j-1,n-1}. \quad (2.4)$$

Thus, (2.4) can be used instead of (2.3a) to express the policy in conjunction with (2.3b).

In many practical cases suppliers choose their order inventory position just as a function of the order history; i.e., they use a policy with an order-inventory kernel, H, that is independent of the current order inventory or, equivalently, where the argument $N_{j,n}$ does not appear in (2.1) or (2.2). Such policies will be called *order-based*. If a policy is order-based, then (2.4) does not include any inventory information. Therefore (2.4) can be iterated by itself, without reference to (2.3b) to develop an order sequence; i.e., orders are just a function of the order history.

Where the *H*-kernel only involves the inventory, a policy will be called *inventory-based*. In this case too (2.3) can be reduced to an inventory-only recursion, based on the inventory history of the downstream supplier. This is done by taking first differences in (2.3b) with respect to j, i.e., $K_{j,n+1} - K_{j-1,n+1} = H_j(K_{j,n}) - H_{j-1}(K_{j-1,n}) - (Q_{j-1,n} - Q_{j-2,n})$, and then replacing the last term with an inventory difference, using the conservation equation. The result is $K_{j,n+1} - K_{j-1,n+1} = H_j(K_{j,n}) - H_{j-1}(K_{j-1,n}) - (K_{j-1,n+1} - K_{j-1,n})$, which reduces to:

$$K_{j,n+1} = H_j(K_{j,n}) - H_{j-1}(K_{j-1,n}) + K_{j-1,n}. \tag{2.5}$$

In an autonomous operation supplier j-1 does not provide inventory information, and supplier j could not use (2.5). Nonetheless, this identity can sometimes be used for analysis.

2.2 Examples

This subsection includes a few examples that illustrate how conventional schemes fit within the proposed framework, and also introduces additional policy classifications: linear and non-linear; smooth and non-smooth.

Example 2.1 (Base-stock policies): The simplest autonomous policy has a constant kernel, γ:

$$N_{j,n+1} = N_{j-1,n} + \gamma. \tag{2.6}$$

This policy is both order-based and inventory-based because its kernel is independent of both inventories and orders. The order-inventory canonical form (2.3) is:

$$Q_{j,n} = \gamma - K_{j,n} \tag{2.7a}$$

$$K_{j,n+1} = \gamma - Q_{j-1,n}. \tag{2.7b}$$

Equation (2.7a) shows that this policy is the "periodic review, order-up-to-level (R, S) system" with order level γ. Note as well that, since H_j is a constant, the order-only expression (2.4) becomes:

$$Q_{j,n} = Q_{j-1,n-1}. \tag{2.8}$$

Thus, the policy is a "local base stock policy," with a lag of one interval, where the orders of supplier j are an exact copy of those of j-1. ∎

Example 2.2 (Forecasting): If supplier j forecasts its future demand (from j-1) based on past history and uses the forecast to establish its order inventory position, then its desired order inventory position is always a function of the data used for the forecast. Since the operation is "autonomous" (no information sharing for more than one level) the forecast can only be based on the order history of j-1. Thus, the kernel of such a policy would only include order history data. The simplest kernel of this type is of the form $\gamma + \beta(N_{j-1,n} - N_{j-1,n-B}) = \gamma + \beta(Q_{j-1,n-1} + \dots + Q_{j-1,n-B})$; i.e., where the desired order inventory position is adapted to past demand with a view toward the future using a moving-average rule over B periods. The canonical form of such a policy is:

$$N_{j,n+1} = N_{j-1,n} + \gamma + \beta(N_{j-1,n} - N_{j-1,n-B}) \tag{2.9a}$$

or

$$Q_{j,n} = \gamma + \beta(Q_{j-1,n-1} + \dots + Q_{j-1,n-B}) - K_{j,n} \tag{2.9b}$$

$$K_{j,n+1} = \gamma + \beta(Q_{j-1,n-1} + \dots + Q_{j-1,n-B}) - Q_{j-1,n}. \tag{2.9c}$$

Note as an aside that if $Q_{j-1,n} \approx Q_{j-1,n-2} \approx \dots \approx Q$, then (2.9c) increases with Q for $\beta B > 1$. Thus if $\beta B > 1$, the policy reduces inventories during extended periods of lower demand as one might desire in practice. Note too that, since the policy is order-based, it has an order-only form (2.4), which is:

$$Q_{j,n} = Q_{j-1,n-1} + \beta(Q_{j-1,n-1} - Q_{j-1,n-B-1}) = (1+\beta)Q_{j-1,n-1} - \beta Q_{j-1,n-B-1}. \tag{2.9d}$$

A simple interpolation, this expression can also be obtained by taking first differences with respect to n in (2.9a). ■

Example 2.3 (Inventory-based policies): The simplest inventory-based policy has a linear kernel, $\gamma + \alpha(N_{j,n} - N_{j-1,n}) = \gamma + \alpha K_{j,n}$. Its canonical forms are:

$$N_{j,n+1} = N_{j-1,n} + \gamma + \alpha(N_{j,n} - N_{j-1,n}) \tag{2.10a}$$

and

$$Q_{j,n} = \gamma + \alpha K_{j,n} - K_{j,n} \tag{2.10b}$$

$$K_{j,n+1} = \gamma + \alpha K_{j,n} - Q_{j-1,n}. \tag{2.10c}$$

Assuming that supplier j–1 uses the same policy as j, the inventory-only expression (2.5) is:

$$K_{j,n+1} = \alpha(K_{j,n}-K_{j-1,n}) + K_{j-1,n} = \alpha K_{j,n} + (1-\alpha)K_{j-1,n} \qquad (2.10\text{d})$$

As in Example 2.2, this result can also be obtained by taking first differences (with respect to j) in the canonical form (2.10a). The outcome is again a simple interpolation. ∎

A policy with a linear or smooth kernel will be said to be linear or smooth. The following are examples of non-linear and non-smooth policies.

Example 2.4 (Policies without cancellations): In many applications order cancellations are undesirable. They can be avoided with monotonic policies that always produce non-negative orders if the input orders are non-negative. We see from (2.9d) that the policies of Example 2.2 are monotonic if $\beta \in [-1, 0]$. In general, a policy will be monotonic if its kernel always exceeds or equals $N_{j,n} - N_{j-1,n}$; see (2.1). Thus, if one wished to use a policy with arbitrary β while maintaining monotonicity, the kernel of (2.9a) would have to be changed; e.g., to:

$$max\{\gamma + \beta(N_{j-1,n}-N_{j-1,n-B}) , (N_{j,n}-N_{j-1,n})\} =$$
$$max\{\gamma + \beta(Q_{j-1,n-1} +... + Q_{j-1,n-B}) , K_{j,n} \}. \qquad (2.11\text{a})$$

Note that (2.11a) is a mixed policy. Likewise, the kernel of Example 2.3 could be changed to

$$max\{\gamma + \alpha(N_{j,n} - N_{j-1,n}) , (N_{j,n}-N_{j-1,n})\} = max\{\gamma + \alpha K_{j,n} , K_{j,n}\}, \qquad (2.11\text{b})$$

to ensure monotonicity. ∎

Policies with non-linear kernels, such as (2.11a) and (2.11b), will be said to be non-linear. If the kernel is continuous and piecewise smooth, as it is in these examples, the policy will be said to be "smooth." Since all the transformations relating the functions F_j , H_j and Y_j of equations (2.1-3) are linear, the linearity and/or smoothness of a policy can be established by examining any of these functions. Convenience is the rule. An example of a non-smooth policy is given below.

Example 2.5 (Order point policies): An example of a discontinuous, mixed kernel is

$$\{S \text{ if } (N_{j,n}-N_{j-1,n}) \leq s \text{ ; or } (N_{j,n}-N_{j-1,n}) \text{ otherwise}\} =$$

$$= \{S \text{ if } K_{j,n} \leq s \text{ ; or } K_{j,n} \text{ otherwise}\}. \tag{2.12a}$$

It is assumed that $S \geq s$. If $S \neq s$ (2.12a) has a jump discontinuity at $K_{j,n} = s$. The corresponding order-inventory canonical form is:

$$Q_{j,n} = S - K_{j,n} \text{ , } \quad \text{if } K_{j,n} \leq s \text{ ; } \quad \text{and } 0 \text{ otherwise.} \tag{2.12b}$$

$$K_{j,n+1} = S - Q_{j-1,n}, \quad \text{if } K_{j,n} \leq s \text{ ; } \quad \text{and } K_{j,n} - Q_{j-1,n} \text{ otherwise.} \tag{2.12c}$$

If the reorder interval h is small, this is the so-called "order point, order-up-to-level (s, S) policy". ∎

All the policies discussed so far, with generic expression (2.1-3), are rooted in history. They will be called *historical* or *non-anticipative* because their input data comes from the past. Even though the goal of adaptation terms such as those used in Example 2.2 may be to forecast the future, the name "non-anticipative" is used because the forecasts can never be assumed to be perfect. The term "*anticipative*" will be reserved for commitment-based policies that allow suppliers to anticipate the future perfectly by agreeing to future demand levels with their clients. Before examining how these policies would work it is convenient to introduce the concept of a "stencil." Stencils are sets of arrows on the on the (t, j)-plane that precisely portray the causality structure of a policy. Arrows rooted at input points, point to the output. Figure 2.2a shows the generic stencil of a mixed, autonomous, non-anticipative policy (2.1-3).

2.3 Anticipative (commitment-based) policies

A more general form of (2.1-3) would include anticipated data. If supplier j knows the orders in A future periods because supplier $j-1$ has committed itself to specific order quantities, then it is possible to use an anticipative kernel, $F_j(N_{j,n} , N_{j-1,n+A} , N_{j-1,n+A-1}, N_{j-1,n+A-2}...)$. Thus, equations (2.1-2) become:

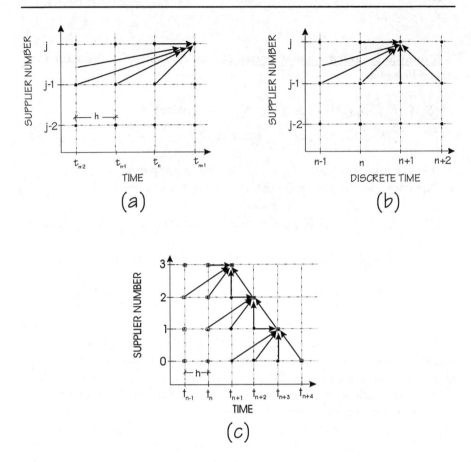

Figure 2.2. Stencils for different discrete-time, autonomous algorithms: (a) Non-anticipative, pull stencil; (b) Anticipative, pull stencil with $A=2$; (c) Influence diagram for anticipative, pull algorithm with $J=3$ and $A=2$ (solid dots = cumulative counts determined by time n; circled dots = cumulative counts realized by time n).

$$N_{j,n+1} = N_{j-1,n} + F_j(N_{j,n}, N_{j-1,n+A}, N_{j-1,n+A-1}, N_{j-1,n+A-2}\ldots, N_{j-1,n+A-B}), \quad (2.13)$$

$$Q_{j,n} = Y_j(N_{j,n}, N_{j-1,n+A}, N_{j-1,n+A-1}, N_{j-1,n+A-2}\ldots, N_{j-1,n+A-B}), \quad (2.14)$$

where Ah is the commitment/anticipation interval. Figure 2.2b depicts the stencil for a rule with $A = 2$. The order-inventory canonical form (2.3) is now:

$$Q_{j,n} = H_j(K_{j,n}, Q_{j-1,n+A-1}, Q_{j-1,n+A-2}, \ldots, Q_{j,n+A-B}) - K_{j,n}, \qquad (2.15a)$$

$$K_{j,n+1} = H_j(K_{j,n}, Q_{j-1,n+A-1}, Q_{j-1,n+A-2}, \ldots, Q_{j,n+A-B}) - Q_{j-1,n}. \qquad (2.15b)$$

If all the suppliers use rule (2.13), then to fulfill its commitment to j, supplier $j-1$ would need commitments from $j-2$, and $j-2$ from $j-3$, etc. The stencils of Fig. 2.2c show how such a chain would work. Solid dots denote the N-values known immediately after time t_n, circled dots the values that are past history, and squared dots the values that just became committed. When the clock advances by one tick, the stencils are shifted to the right by one lattice spacing, and the customer adds one order at the end of its horizon. With this information and the new stencil, supplier 1 places a new order, which allows supplier 2 to do the same, etc. The key requirement in this scheme is that once a future order has been placed it cannot be changed.

The figure clearly shows that if a chain has J suppliers with the same anticipation, then the "customer" would have to commit itself for $1 + (A-1)J$ periods; i.e., the commitment horizon for the chain is:

$$\text{Commitment horizon} = [1 + (A-1)J]h. \qquad (2.16)$$

If the customer is not willing to cooperate, one can ask the first supplier to keep safety stocks and play the role of customer.[3] For simplicity of notation, if a lead supplier is used it will be labeled $j = 0$, and its orders will become the input to our analysis, $N_0(t)$. This is a valid simplification for stability analysis since, as was mentioned in Sec. 1.1, the stability properties pertain to infinite chains with arbitrary inputs.

The idea of using commitments to enhance the operation of a supply chain is nothing new. Commitments are required to run just-in-time (JIT) chains, and we will see later in these notes that JIT systems are a special case of (2.13 - 2.15).

Example 2.6 (Commitment-based policies): Two examples of anticipative policies, expressed in canonical form (2.13), are:

(a) Order-based: $N_{j,n+1} = \gamma + N_{j-1,n+A} + \beta(N_{j-1,n+A} - N_{j-1,n-B})$ (2.17a)

---

[3] In both cases the committing entity must be compensated for its added expense with cheaper prices. This should be possible because as we shall see later in these notes total savings for long chains are usually larger than the commitment penalty.

(*b*) Mixed: $N_{j,n+1} = \gamma + \alpha\,N_{j,n} + (1 - \alpha)N_{j-1,n+A}.$ (2.17b)

Their kernels, F_j, are obtained by subtracting $N_{j-1,n}$ from the right sides. Policy (2.17b) is related to the ACT policy, discussed later in these notes. The connection will become clear later. It will be convenient to write below the expression for its order size – by subtracting $N_{j,n}$ from both sides of (2.17b):

(*b*) Mixed: $Q_{j,n} = \gamma - (1-\alpha)(N_{j,n} - N_{j-1,n+A}).$ ∎   (2.17c)

2.4 Flexible commitment policies

A disadvantage of commitment-based algorithms is the rigidity of the commitments required of every supplier. Another disadvantage of smooth policies (such as those in Examples 2.1, 2.2 and 2.4) is that they require a shipment in every interval. This may not be desirable when h is small. Introducing some flexibility into the commitment process, as explained below, can eliminate these drawbacks. The new policies will be called "flex-time" or "flexible commitment" policies. They are particularly attractive when suppliers produce many different items as part of a network because the added flexibility allows the suppliers to schedule more efficient production runs.

The policies work as follows. An anticipative algorithm like (2.13) is used to obtain upper bounds, $U_j(t_n)$, for the cumulative orders placed by each supplier, instead of the orders themselves. Suppliers are then allowed to place orders of any size without forewarning (at times not necessarily on the lattice) provided $N_j(t) \le U_j(t)$ for all t; see Fig. 2.3. To ensure reliability, lower bounds, $V_j(t)$, are also defined for the orders. The lower bounds can be chosen in any way, but we require $U_j(t) \ge V_j(t) \ge U_{j-1}(t+M_j)$. (This happens in Fig. 2.3 if we assume that $M_j \le h$.) These inequalities ensure reliability, because then $N_j(t) \ge V_j(t) \ge U_{j-1}(t+M_j) \ge N_{j-1}(t+M_j)$, in agreement with (1.5).

Flex-time algorithms in which suppliers place an order whenever $N_j(t) = V_j(t)$ are also related to order-point inventory control methods. The only difference is that in a flex-time method the trigger is based on the bounds U_{j-1} of the downstream supplier, rather than on the orders themselves. This is a logical approach since with the built-in flexibility the downstream supplier may choose to bring its orders up to the maximum level at any time.

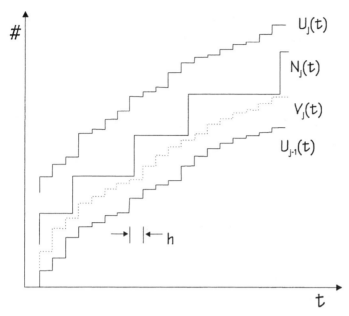

Figure 2.3. Bounds and *N*-curves for a flex-time system.

2.5 Policies for queuing systems and traffic flow

Serial queuing systems are similar to supply chains, in that customers (items) flow from one server (supplier) j to the next, $j-1$, obeying strict conservation laws. In these systems "orders" flow together with the physical items, so there is no need for distinguishing between the N- and S-curves. In bulk queuing systems customers arrive at a station in groups and are also processed in groups. Like supply chains, queuing systems can be operated in discrete or continuous time. The discrete approach is used here without loss of generality. Customers that have arrived at a server but have not yet been processed are said to be queued (inventoried) at that server. Customers may also have to spend a handling time (or "service time") at each station, and a travel time between servers. The sum of the two is analogous to the "processing time" of a supply chain. Servers usually have a "capacity" to process a maximum number of customers in each time interval. This capacity may depend on the number of customers in the queue, and on the history of the queue, if the system is managed dynamically; e.g., when the serving workforce is increased if the queue becomes too long. Therefore, the number of customers served by $j-1$ in the interval $(n, n+1)$, $Q_{j-1,n}$, can usually be expressed as a function of the prior customer departures from j, and the current queue. In terms of cumulative Newell curves of customer departures, this is:

$$Q_{j-1,n+1} = Y_{j-1}(N_{j-1,n}, N_{j,n}, N_{j,n-1}, N_{j,n-2} \ldots N_{j,n-B}). \tag{2.18}$$

This expression is similar to (2.2) except for an inverted stencil. See Fig. 2.4a and compare with Fig. 2.2a.

In most queuing systems items cannot be processed until after they have arrived. Therefore, physically valid instances of (2.18) must have this property. If we let M_j be the processing time between j and $j-1$ of a queuing system, the validity condition is simply (1.5). Thus, we see that the reliability of supply chains is connected with the feasibility of queuing rules.

A queuing rule should also be "proper", and therefore, should also be expressible in a canonical form similar to (2.3) that only involves the queue at $j-1$, $K_{j-1,n} = N_{j,n} - N_{j-1,n}$, and the order history from j. Similar manipulations reveal that the canonical form is now:

$$Q_{j-1,n} = H_{j-1}(K_{j-1,n}, Q_{j,n-1}, \ldots, Q_{j,n-B}) + K_{j-1,n} \tag{2.19a}$$

$$K_{j-1,n+1} = -H_{j-1}(K_{j-1,n}, Q_{j,n-1}, \ldots, Q_{j,n-B}) + Q_{j,n}, \tag{2.19b}$$

where the negative of the H-kernel is the queue that server $j-1$ would have at time $n+1$ if there were to be no further arrivals ($Q_{j,n} = 0$). The only reason for the sign reversals between expressions (2.19) and (2.3) is that queues play the mathematical role of "negative inventories". (If we had defined $K_{j-1,n} = -N_{j,n} + N_{j-1,n}$, then the equations would have been perfectly symmetrical.)

Blocking: In systems with closely spaced servers there may be limited storage space for queues, and customers may be prevented from departing a station if they are blocked by a spillover from a downstream server. These systems should obviously be modeled with a kernel that includes information from the downstream server. The stencil for a queuing system with blocking would be as in Fig. 2.4b.

Traffic flow: Freeways systems have been modeled as a queuing network with blocking (e.g., Daganzo, 1994). In these models the freeway is partitioned into small cells with an ability to store a given number of stopped vehicles, separated by imaginary servers with a given "capacity" to process vehicles per unit time. This can be done in various ways depending on the specific macroscopic effects that one wishes to achieve. [In steady but congested—or blocked—traffic vehicles space themselves farther apart when the "flow" passing through the cell (in vehicles per unit time) is higher. Therefore the maximum number of vehicles in a cell should decline with flow when traffic is blocked. This is one of the above mentioned macroscopic effects.] Figures 2.4c and d present two different stencils that have been proposed (Newell, 1993, Daganzo, 1993 and 1995, and also Lebacque, 1993). These models have been tested against real data with relatively good results (e.g., White et al, 1998, Hurdle and Son, 2000). When traffic is blocked only the downstream part of the stencil is used. (This is the special case that turns out to be most relevant for supply chains.) The formulas for blocked traffic corresponding to Figs. 2.4c and d are:

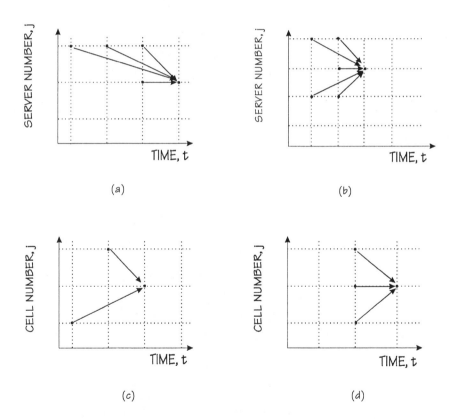

Figure 2.4. Stencils for queuing and traffic models: (a) queuing; (b) queuing with blocking; (c) traffic-1 (Newell, with *B*=1); (d) traffic-2 (cell-transmission).

$$N_{j,n+1} = \gamma + N_{j-1,n-B} \qquad \text{(Newell, order-based).} \qquad (2.20a)$$

$$N_{j,n+1} = N_{j,n} + Y_j(N_{j,n} - N_{j-1,n}) \quad \text{(Cell-transmission, inventory-based)} \qquad (2.20b)$$

where Y_j is a user-defined monotonic function that should decrease at a rate greater than or equal to -1. Note that (2.20a) is the special case of Example 2.2 with $\beta = -1$, and (2.20b) is a non-linear version of Example 2.3. (The example corresponds to $Y_j(K_{j,n}) = \gamma + (\alpha - 1)K_{j,n}$.) Equations (2.20) will turn out to be relevant for supply chain management because they have desirable stability properties, and can be used as a guide to construct useful inventory management policies. We will return to these ideas in Chapter 5. The following chapter examines what "proper" policies should and should not do.

3. Algorithmic Properties

This chapter focuses on the behavior of possible policies. It first introduces in Sec. 2.1 two additional properties that a policy must satisfy in order to avoid pathological behavior of one form or another, i.e., to be truly proper, and then examines (in Sec. 2.2) key properties of proper policies.

3.1 Properness

We have already noted that for a policy to be *proper* the output of its kernel F_j should be independent of which order is labeled "zero," and that as a result all autonomous proper policies have an order-inventory canonical form (2.15). Two more requirements of a proper algorithm are: (i) that it should produce bounded order sizes and inventories for supplier j if the orders from $j-1$ are bounded, and (ii) that the time-average of these inventories (or any other statistic of the sequence) should not depend on the initial conditions if the orders from $j-1$ are constant. The first requirement (*boundedness*) is obviously necessary. The second requirement (*ergodicity*) is also logical, if a policy is to be of practical use. If it was not true, then the character of the inventory sequence experienced by a supplier during an infinitely long season with steady demand Q could depend on a finite pre-history with variable demand. This is undesirable since finite causes should not have infinite effects.

The properness/improperness of a policy can often be established by inspection. For example, rule (2.10) is obviously improper if $\alpha > 1$. The rule is improper because the sequence $\{K_{j,n}\}$ generated by (2.10c) diverges under conditions of zero demand if $\alpha > 1$. Two sufficient conditions for boundedness and ergodicity are developed below. Note that these tests neither imply nor assume monotonicity.

Boundedness test: Let the input order sequence for a supplier, j, be bounded by $|Q_{j-1,n}| \le |Q_{max}|$. The supplier's policy produces bounded inventories and orders if for any valid set of arguments its H-kernel satisfies:

$$\left| H_j(K_{j,n} , Q_{j-1,n+A-1} , \dots , Q_{j-1, n+A-B}) \right| \leq \pi_0 \left| K_{j,n} \right| + \pi_1 \tag{3.1}$$

for some $0 \leq \pi_0 < 1$ and $\pi_1 < \infty$ that could depend on Q_{max}. ■

Proof: We first establish that if (3.1) holds the resulting inventory sequence $\{K_{j,n}\}$ is bounded. Note from (2.15b) that

$$\left| K_{j,n+1} \right| \leq \left| H_j(K_{j,n} , Q_{j-1,n+A-1} , \dots , Q_{j-1, n+A-B}) \right| + \left| Q_{j-1,n} \right|.$$

Inserting (3.1) into this expression and recognizing that $\left| Q_{j-1,n} \right| \leq \left| Q_{max} \right|$ we find:

$$\left| K_{j,n+1} \right| \leq \pi_0 \left| K_{j,n} \right| + \pi_1 + \left| Q_{max} \right|.$$

If $\left| K_{j,n} \right|$ is now replaced by its upper bound, $\pi_0 \left| K_{j,n-1} \right| + \pi_1 + \left| Q_{max} \right|$, we obtain:

$$\left| K_{j,n+1} \right| \leq \pi_0^2 \left| K_{j,n-1} \right| + (1+\pi_0)(\pi_1 + \left| Q_{max} \right|).$$

Repetition of this procedure yields:

$$\left| K_{j,n+1} \right| \leq \pi_0^{n+1} \left| K_{j,0} \right| + (1+\pi_0+\pi_0^2+\dots+\pi_0^n)(\pi_1 + \left| Q_{max} \right|).$$

The two terms of this expression are bounded since $|\pi_0| < 1$. Thus $\{K_{j,n}\}$ is bounded.

To see that the output order sequence $\{Q_{j,n}\}$ is also bounded let the inventory bound be M and introduce (3.1) in (2.15a). The result shows that:

$$Q_{j,n} \leq \pi_0 \left| K_{j,n} \right| + \pi_1 - K_{j,n} \leq \pi_0 M + \pi_1 + M.$$

Thus, $\{Q_{j,n}\}$ is also bounded. ■

An ergodicity test is given below. Since the input orders are constant, it is convenient to define from (2.15b) the function, h_Q, that returns the new inventory as a function of the old when the input order size is Q; i.e.,: $h_Q(K) = H_j(K, Q, \dots , Q) - Q$.

Ergodicity test: If h_Q has a fixed point $K_{eq,Q}$ for all Q, and in all cases satisfies the following contraction property, $\left| h_Q(K) - h_Q(K_{eq,Q}) \right| \leq \pi_{0,Q} \left| K - K_{eq,Q} \right|$ for some $0 \leq \pi_{0,Q} < 1$ and all Q, then the policy is ergodic. ■

Proof: Since $K_{eq,Q}$ is a fixed point, the contraction property can be written as $\left| h_Q(K) - K_{eq,Q} \right| \le \pi_{0,Q} \left| K - K_{eq,Q} \right|$. Therefore, $\left| K_{j,n+1} - K_{eq,Q} \right| \le \pi_{0,Q} \left| K_{j,n} - K_{eq,Q} \right|$. This ensures that the sequence $\{K_{j,n} - K_{eq,Q}\}$ converges to 0 for all Q; i.e., that $\{K_{j,n}\}$ converges to $K_{eq,Q}$ independent of the initial conditions. Therefore $\{K_{j,n}\}$ is ergodic. ∎

Since the kernel of order-based policies does not depend on K, these policies pass the boundedness test (with $\pi_0 = 0$) if their kernel is bounded for any set of valid (bounded) Q's. This will happen, for example, if the kernel is continuous. The ergodicity test is also passed by all order-based policies because $h_Q(K)$ is then a constant, and therefore $h_Q(K) = K_{eq,Q}$ for all K. The test is obviously passed with $\pi_{0,Q} = 0$. Hence we have just shown that all smooth, order-based policies (e.g., Examples 2.1, 2.2 and 2.6a) are proper.

It is now shown that inventory-based policies are proper if their kernel $H_j(K)$ is continuous and monotone with a maximum absolute rate of variation, $0 \le \pi_a < 1$. This assertion implies that the policy of Example 2.3 is proper if $-1 < \alpha < 1$. To prove the assertion, note first that $\left| H_j(K) - H_j(0) \right| \le \pi_a \left| K \right|$, since the rate of variation is bounded by π_a in the interval $[0, K]$. Hence $\left| H_j(K) \right| \le \pi_a \left| K \right| + \left| H_j(0) \right|$; i.e., the boundedness test is satisfied with $\pi_0 = \pi_a$ and $\pi_1 = \left| H_j(0) \right|$. Note too that $h_Q(K) = H_j(K) - Q$ is also continuous and monotone, with the same rate of variation as H_j. As such, it must have a fixed point $K_{eq,Q}$. Furthermore, its absolute variation in an interval with end points K and $K_{eq,Q}$ must satisfy $\left| h_Q(K) - h_Q(K_{eq,Q}) \right| \le \pi_a \left| K - K_{eq,Q} \right|$, since its absolute rate of variation is still bounded by π_a. Thus, the policy passes the ergodicity test with $\pi_{0,Q} = \pi_a$.

It is also possible to show using similar arguments that smooth, mixed policies for which $\left| \partial H_j(K_{j,n}, Q_{j-1,n+A-1}, \ldots, Q_{j-1,n+A-B})/\partial K_{j,n} \right| \le \pi_0 < 1$ are proper. Hence, the mixed policy of Example 2.6b, given by (2.17b), is proper if $-1 < \alpha < 1$.

It should be stressed that the tests are only sufficient conditions. There are policies that fail the tests but can be shown to be proper under certain conditions. An example is the order point policy, (2.12), which fails the ergodicity test because it does not have a fixed point if $Q < (S - s)$,[1] but is bounded and ergodic nonetheless for non-negative orders. If $Q_{j-1,n} \ge 0$, (2.12c) shows that $K_{j,n+1} \in [S - Q_{max}, S]$ for all n. Hence the inventories are bounded. This implies that the orders are also bounded, as can be seen by

---

[1] The policy cannot have a fixed point because according to (2.12c) the equilibrium inventory would have to equal $K_{eq,Q} = S - Q$ and satisfy $K_{eq,Q} \le s$. This, however, is impossible, if $Q < (S - s)$ because then $K_{eq,Q} \equiv S - Q > S - (S - s) = s$.

combining the inventory bound with (2.12b) to reveal that $Q_{j,n} \in [0, Q_{max}]$ for all n. Thus, the policy is bounded. The policy is also ergodic because under conditions of steady demand, the orders and inventories repeat themselves in a unique way with a period of $\lceil (S-s)/Q \rceil$ intervals. The pattern is as follows: when a positive order is placed the order inventory position becomes S. The inventory then declines by Q units every interval, until the inventory reaches the trigger point, s. This happens after $\lceil (S-s)/Q \rceil$ intervals. An order is then placed and the pattern is repeated. Figure 3.1 illustrates the behavior of the policy, both, when $Q < (S-s)$ and when $(S-s) \leq Q \leq S$. (The steps of the N_{j-1} curve have been smoothed in the figure.) Note that if the input order size exceeds S the policy violates condition (1.5).

3.2 Steady-state properties

A steady state (or equilibrium) is said to exist for a given policy and order size Q if (2.13) has a solution with parallel N-curves and steps, Q, as in Fig. 3.2a. The vertical separation between curves is the steady state inventory for the given order size. This section characterizes the steady state behavior of autonomous policies, and introduces some of their properties.

The existence of a steady state cannot be taken for granted, even for proper policies. Recall that policy (2.12) is proper but does not have a steady state if $Q < (S-s)$ as illustrated in Fig. 3.1a. Recall too that policy (2.12) is discontinuous. The following result describes the connection between properness, smoothness, and steady state behavior.

Theorem 3.1 (Existence and Uniqueness of a Steady State): If a policy is proper and smooth, then: (i) it must have a unique steady state for every Q, and (ii) the inventory sequence under a steady input always tends to the unique equilibrium, independent of the initial conditions. ∎

Proof: We prove the existence part (i) by a construction argument. Consider the sequence $\{K_{j,n} | Q, K_{j,0}\}$ generated by a particular Q and $K_{j,0}$ with the recursion implied by (2.15b), $K_{j,n+1} = H_j(K_{j,n}, Q, \ldots) - Q \equiv h_Q(K_{j,n})$. This sequence is bounded because the policy is proper. Assume for now that the sequence is monotonic so that it converges to a limit, $K_{eq,Q}$. In this case, if we take limits on both sides of $K_{j,n+1} = h_Q(K_{j,n})$, we see that $K_{eq,Q} = h_Q(K_{eq,Q})$ because h_Q is continuous. Thus, a steady state, $K_{eq,Q}$, exists if the

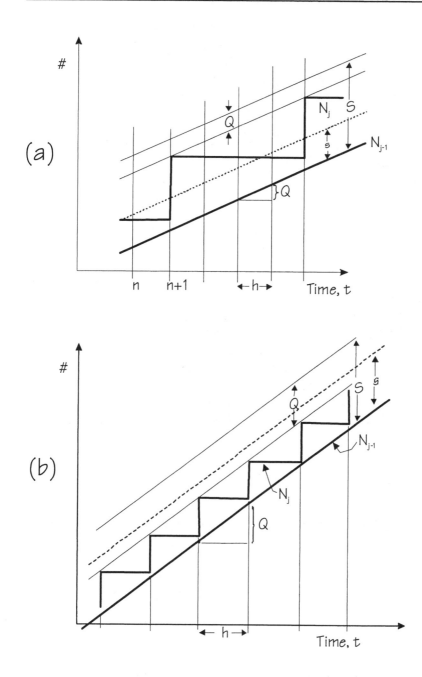

Figure 3.1. Behavior of the (S, s) policy with steady demand: (a) $Q < (S\text{-}s)$; (b) $(S\text{-}s) \le Q \le S$

sequence is monotonic. If the sequence is not monotone, there must be two jumps in the sequence, $K_{j,n+1} - K_{j,n} \equiv h_Q(K_{j,n}) - K_{j,n}$, with opposite signs for two different $K_{j,n}$'s. Since h_Q is continuous, this implies that the equation $0 = h_Q(K) - K$ must have a root, $K_{eq,Q}$, for a value of K between the two $K_{j,n}$.'s. Thus, an equilibrium inventory can also be identified if the sequence is not monotonic. Hence, a steady state always exists.

Uniqueness follows from ergodicity. If the steady state equation $K = h_Q(K)$ were to have two (or more) different solutions, then the two inventory sequences generated with these values as starting points would have different long run averages (equal to the starting values). But this is impossible because the policy is ergodic. Hence (i) is proven.

Point (ii) also follows from ergodicity since ergodicity implies that all sequences must have the same long run statistics as the sequence started with the unique equilibrium inventory. ∎

_K_-functions of smooth policies: It will be convenient from now on to drop the subscript "_eq_" and denote the steady state inventory of a supplier, _j_, simply by K_j; e.g. as in Fig 3.2a. The subscript "_j_" may itself be dropped when differentiation across suppliers is not needed. Theorem 3.1 showed that the steady state inventory of a supplier operating with a smooth, proper policy is uniquely determined by its input order size. Thus, we can define a function, $K_j = \kappa_j(Q)$, to embody this relationship. This function will be called the "_κ_-function" of the (smooth, proper) policy. Because in practical applications it is more physically meaningful to relate the steady state inventory of a policy to the demand rate in continuous time, $q = Q/h$, we also define a "_K_-function", $K_j(q) = \kappa_j(qh)$.

The reader can verify that the _κ_- and _K_-functions of the smooth proper policies in Examples 2.1-4 and 2.6 are:

$$K(Q/h) = \kappa(Q) = \gamma - Q \qquad \text{for example 2.1} \qquad (3.2a)$$

$$= \gamma + (\beta B - 1)Q \qquad \text{for example 2.2} \qquad (3.2b)$$

$$= (\gamma - Q)/(1-\alpha) \qquad \text{for example 2.3} \qquad (3.2c)$$

$$= \gamma + (\beta B - 1)Q \qquad \text{for example 2.4a } (Q > 0) \quad (3.2d)$$

$$= (\gamma - Q)/(1-\alpha) \qquad \text{for example 2.4b } (Q > 0) \quad (3.2e)$$

$$= \gamma + (\beta(B+A) + A - 1)Q \qquad \text{for example 2.6a} \qquad (3.2f)$$

$$= AQ + (\gamma - Q)/(1-\alpha) \qquad \text{for example 2.6b.} \qquad (3.2g)$$

It is generally true that linear policies have linear κ-functions, as occurs in these examples. Non-linear kernels lead to non-linear κ-functions, however.

Example 3.1 (Non-linear κ-function): An example of an order-based, smooth, proper policy with a non-linear κ-function is defined by the following H-kernel:

$$\gamma + Q_{j-1,n-1} + \beta(Q_{j-1,n-1} + ... + Q_{j-1,n-B})^{\frac{1}{2}}. \tag{3.3a}$$

The policy is well defined only for monotone inputs. It is proper because it is order-based. Its κ-function is:

$$K(Q/h) = \kappa(Q) = \gamma + \beta(BQ)^{\frac{1}{2}}. \quad \blacksquare \tag{3.3b}$$

Finally note that the K- and κ-functions of smooth, proper policies are always smooth. This is true because they are implicit functions defined by a smooth steady state equation, $K = H_j(K, Q, ...) - Q$.

Gain and linearity: Figure 3.2b shows a hypothetical K-function. Its intercept, K_o, is the order inventory that would arise during an extended period of zero demand. Its slope has units of time. It represents the change in the equilibrium inventory for a small change in demand, and will be called the "gain", g. The derivative of the κ-function, $G = g/h$, also measures gain, but does so in terms of the number of intervals; it will be called the "dimensionless gain." Since, as a rule, suppliers prefer to keep lower inventories during low-demand seasons, practical algorithms should have non-negative gains. This happens for our examples if the gains G obtained from (3.2) and (3.3b) satisfy:

$(\beta B - 1) \geq 0$	for example 2.2 and 2.4a	(3.4a)
$-1/(1-\alpha) \geq 0$	for example 2.3 and 2.4b	(3.4b)
$\beta(B+A) + A - 1 \geq 0$	for example 2.6a	(3.4c)
$A - 1/(1-\alpha) \geq 0$	for example 2.6b	(3.4d)
$\frac{1}{2}\beta B(BQ)^{-\frac{1}{2}} \geq 0$	for example 3.1.	(3.4e)

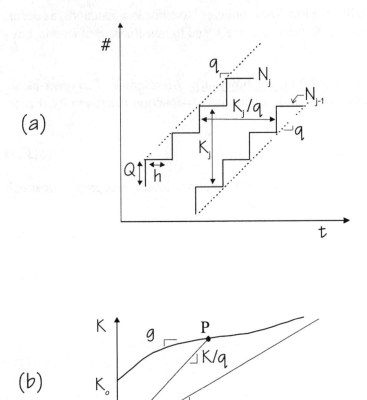

Figure 3.2. Steady state diagrams: (a) N-curves; (b) A feasible K-function

Recall that inventory-based Examples 2.3 and 2.4b are proper only if $\alpha \in$ (–1, 1). Thus, these policies cannot achieve positive gains. The non-linear κ-function of Example 3.1 has a positive gain only if $\beta > 0$. Note too that linear policies have constant gains, since their κ-functions are linear.

Reliability: In practice, we should also be interested in ascertaining whether the steady states achieved by a policy are reliable in the sense of (1.5). This can be determined graphically from a picture of the κ- or K-function in a neat way; see Fig. 3.2b. The figure shows that the slope of a ray joining a point, "P", on the K-curve with the origin equals K/q. Figure

3.2a shows that (for supplier j) this ratio is the horizontal separation between curves N_j and N_{j-1} for the given steady state. The steady state is reliable, according to (1.5), if this separation exceeds or equals M_j; i.e., if as occurs on Fig. 3.2b, point "P" lies on or above a ray with slope M_j from the origin. A policy with reliable steady states for the range of q's that can occur ($0 \leq q \leq q_{max}$) is said to have a reliable K-function; this happens if the K-curve lies above the ray with slope M_j. Of course, it still remains to be determined whether a reliable K-function implies a reliable operation in the dynamic case.

4. Stability and Monotonicity Requirements

This chapter examines how gain and the anticipation level of commitment-based policies affect the stability and monotonicity of homogeneous supply chains; i.e., chains where suppliers use the same policy: $F_j \equiv F, H_j \equiv H$. Stability and monotonicity are desirable properties, but separate issues. Instability can lead to the bullwhip effect, and lack of monotonicity to order cancellations. Therefore, they are studied separately. Section 4.1 defines the two forms of stability considered in these notes, "stability in the small" and "stability in the large", and their connection with the bullwhip effect. Sec. 4.2 develops a stability test, which is illustrated with several examples in Sec. 4.3. A monotonicity test for order-based policies is then presented in Sec. 4.4. Together, Sections 4.1-4 show that historical policies (without commitments) and positive gains are problematic, both, from the standpoint of stability and monotonicity. Since as a rule, suppliers prefer policies with positive gain, this explains the prevalence of the bullwhip effect. The last section of the chapter (Sec. 4.5) extends the results to queuing systems.

4.1 Types of stability

We say that a policy is *stable in the small* if the deviations from a steady state Q across the whole chain can be bounded uniformly as tightly as desired by bounding the deviations in the input. More precisely, a policy is stable in the small if for every Q there is a positive δ_o, possibly very small, such that for all $\delta \in (0, \delta_o]$, there is a $\delta' \in (0, \delta]$ such that:

$$\{|Q_{0,n} - Q| \le \delta', \forall n\} \Rightarrow \{|Q_{j,n} - Q| \le \delta, \forall j, n\} \text{ (stability in the small) (4.1)}$$

Stability in the small implies that arbitrarily small deviations from a steady order rate can be maintained for an entire supply chain by steadying the demand input. Policies that are stable in the small will be said to be in the class S.

We say that a policy is *"stable in the large,"* belongs to class *L*, if for every positive δ', no matter how large, there is a δ such that:

$$\{|Q_{0,n}| \le \delta', \forall\, n\} \;\Rightarrow\; \{|Q_{j,n}| \le \delta, \;\forall\, j, n\} \quad \text{(stability in the large.)} \qquad (4.2)$$

Stability in the large guarantees that the order sizes of an infinite chain are bounded if the input orders are bounded. Policies not in *L* are said to suffer from the bullwhip effect.

Similar definitions could be given based on the behavior of the inventories, but this is not necessary since policies that are stable (unstable) with respect to order size turn out to be stable (unstable) with respect to inventories. This should be clear for stability in the large, because the boundedness property of proper policies implies that inventories are bounded if orders are bounded. It will be shown to be true for stability in the small in Sec. 4.2.

Figure 4.1a shows that *S* and *L* are not related in any particular way, in the general non-linear case. Policies in $S \cap L$ are said to be *strongly stable*. Policies exist that are in *L* but not in *S*, and vice versa. An example of each type is given below. However, *S* and *L* are equivalent in the linear case. This is shown in Fig. 4.1b and demonstrated in Sec. 4.2. This section also shows how to check if a policy is in *S*. Figure 4.1b shows that tests for membership in *S* also establish strong stability in the linear case. In the non-linear case, however, additional ad-hoc tests are needed to check membership in *L*.

Figure 4.1 also shows a set H^+, in the unstable region. This is the set of historical (non-anticipative) policies with positive gain. It will be argued in Sec. 4.3 that all policies in H^+ should lie outside the stability region, and therefore must suffer the bullwhip effect. We will also learn in Sec. 4.4 that policies in H^+ generate order cancellations.

Example 4.1 (Policy in $\{L-S\}$): Order point strategies (Example 2.5) are an example of policies that are stable in the large but not in the small. We saw at the end of Sec 3.1 that the inventories and orders of these policies are uniformly bounded, if the customer orders are non-negative. Thus, any such policy is in *L*. For these policies, however, a steady input with order size $Q = (S-s)/2$ yields output orders of alternating sizes, 0 and $S-s$. Since any infinitesimal perturbation to such an input stream changes some of the positive orders to 0, we see that there cannot be a $\delta' > 0$ for which (4.1) holds. Hence, order point policies are not in *S*. ■

Example 4.2 (Policy in {$S-L$}): Some non-linear, order-based policies belong to this category. Because they are order-based, they can be expressed in the order-only form (2.4); e.g. as we did with (linear) Example 2.2. A non-linear example is:

$$Q_{j,n} = Q_{j-1,n-1}, \text{ if } |Q_{j-1,n-1} - Q_{j,n-2}| \leq \delta_0 \ll 1, \quad \text{p3072X} \tag{4.3a}$$

$$= Q_{j-1,n-1} + (Q_{j-1,n-1} - Q_{j,n-2}), \qquad \text{otherwise} \tag{4.3b}$$

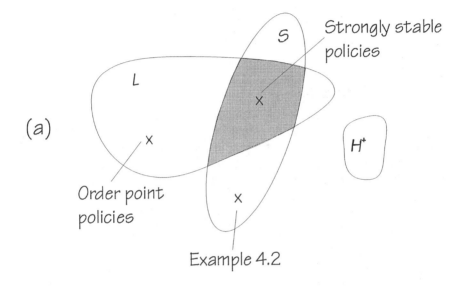

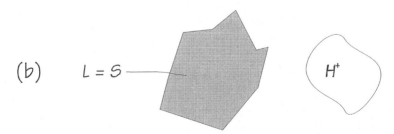

Figure 4.1. Venn diagram for autoÿomous policies: (a) nonlinear case; (b) linear case.

This is the same policy as (2.9d) with $B = 1$, if the coefficient β is allowed to take the values 0 or 1, depending on the magnitude of $(Q_{j-1,n-1} - Q_{j-1,n-2})$.

Consideration shows that when the customer series $\{Q_{0,n}\}$ deviates little from a steady state, equation (4.3a) holds for all suppliers ($j = 1, 2 \ldots$), and all suppliers experience the same order sequence (with a lag). Obviously then, (4.1) holds with $\delta' = \delta$ and the system is stable in the small. However, the system is not stable to large perturbations. If the customer order sequence alternates as follows, $\{\ldots 0, 1, 0, 1, \ldots\}$, then (4.3) reveals that supplier 1 will place the alternating order sequence $\{\ldots -1, 2, -1, 2, \ldots\}$, supplier 2 the sequence $\{\ldots 0, 5, 0, 5, \ldots\}$ and supplier 3 the sequence $\{\ldots -5, 10, -5, 10, \ldots\}$. We see that the amplitude of the order fluctuation grows by a factor of 5 when j increases by 2. Thus, the policy suffers the bullwhip effect and cannot be in L. ∎

4.2 Stability analysis

Policies that are not smooth around every steady state, as occurred with Example 4.1, are inherently unstable in the small since they can translate infinitesimal input changes into finite output changes. Therefore the analysis in this section is restricted to policies that are differentiable in the neighborhood of every steady state.[1] The analysis is also restricted to discrete-time policies but its results can be extended to continuous-time simply by letting $h \to 0$. Since the stability conditions turn out to be independent of h, the extension is trivial. Continuous time policies could be of interest with flex-time systems where the bounds, $U_j(t)$, can be constantly updated with a continuous-time version of (2.13).[2] In these cases, stability should be measured by the behavior of the $U_j(t)$.

Since we are interested in tracking infinitesimal perturbations from a steady state solution of of (2.13), given by $[N_{j,n}]_{ss} = \text{constant} + nQ + j\kappa(Q)$, equation (2.13) can be linearized about this steady state and expressed exclusively in terms of the deviations ε_{jn} of $N_{j,n}$ from the steady state. A power series expansion of (2.13) shows that to a first order of approximation the deviations satisfy:

---

[1] The analysis can be extended to policies that are piecewise differentiable, but this would complicate the notation unnecessarily, and therefore it is not done.

[2] Continuous updating is impractical for non-flex-time systems that require orders to be placed every period.

$$\varepsilon_{j,n+1} \cong \alpha\, \varepsilon_{j,n} + \beta_{-A}\varepsilon_{j-1,n+A} + \beta_{1-A}\varepsilon_{j-1,n+A-1} + \ldots \quad (n \text{ integer}; j = 1, \ldots J), \qquad (4.4)$$

where $(\alpha, \beta_{-A}, \beta_{1-A}, \ldots, \beta_{B-A})$ are the partial derivatives of the right side of (2.13) evaluated at the steady state. Equation (4.4) turns out to be exact if the policy is linear. To see this note that in the linear case (2.13) becomes:

$$N_{j,n+1} = \gamma + \alpha N_{j,n} + \beta_{-A}N_{j-1,n+A} + \beta_{1-A}N_{j-1,n+A-1} + \ldots \qquad (4.5)$$

Furthermore, since a valid steady state solution, $[N_{j,n}]_{ss}$, must satisfy (4.5) as an identity, this identity can be subtracted from (4.5). The result of this manipulation is (4.4). Since this expression is now exact, it applies to both large and small perturbations in the linear case.

We now show that stability as determined by an analysis of (4.4) implies that perturbations of all types (i.e., of orders or inventories) are well behaved.

By taking the first forward differences of (2.13) with respect to n and linearizing the result about a steady state, or by taking first differences in (4.5) if the system is linear, we find that the order sizes also obey (4.4); i.e.,

$$Q_{j,n+1} \cong \alpha\, Q_{j,n} + \beta_{-A}Q_{j-1,n+A} + \beta_{1-A}Q_{j-1,n+A-1} + \ldots \quad (n \text{ integer}; j = 1, \ldots J.) \qquad (4.6)$$

This approximation holds if the $Q_{j,n}$ are close to a steady state, Q. In the linear case, however, (4.6) is exact and holds for all $\{Q_{j,n}\}$. In both cases, the steady state Q must satisfy (4.6) as an identity; i.e. $[Q = \alpha Q + \beta_{-A}Q + \beta_{1-A}Q + \ldots]$. This identity implies that if a steady state $Q \neq 0$ exists (i.e., the policy is proper) then the coefficients $(\alpha, \beta_{-A}, \ldots)$ must add to 1, i.e., we need

$$\alpha + \sum_{l=1-A}^{\infty} \beta_l = 1 \qquad \text{(for existence.)} \qquad (4.7)$$

If the identity $[Q = \alpha Q + \beta_{-A}Q + \beta_{1-A}Q + \ldots]$ is now subtracted from both sides of (4.6), the result is again an expression identical to (4.4) that applies to the order size deviations from the steady state.

By subtracting the j and j-1 instances of (2.13) and linearizing the result, or by taking the first differences of (4.5) with respect to j, we find that (4.4) also holds for the inventories and for the inventory deviations. Thus, an analysis of (4.4) is sufficiently general to determine the stability of a policy.

In the following, for notational convenience, we shall use "Q" as the variable name in (4.4); i.e., we shall work with (4.6). We stress, though, that the analysis pertains to the perturbations (of any type); i.e., of order number, N, order size, Q, or inventory, K. Stability is just a property of the vector $(\alpha, \beta_{-A}, \ldots)$. The easiest way to determine stability-in-the-small appears to be with Von Neumann's method, as explained below, but this is not the only way to do it. The reader familiar with control theory might have been inclined to use "frequency-domain" analysis. Appendix A shows that the results with this approach are the same as those about to be derived.

Von Neumann's stability test: We consider here, customer input sequences $\{Q_{0,n}\}$ with a possibly very large, but finite, number of non-zero terms. Since (4.6) defines a linear and homogeneous set of difference equations it should have solutions of the form $Q_{j,n} = \xi(\omega)^j \exp(-n\omega i)$, where ω is real, $\xi(\omega)$ is complex, and i is the imaginary square root of -1. These solutions are called "modes". Linear combinations of modes are also solutions because (4.6) is linear and homogeneous. Furthermore, a linear combination of modes with $\omega \in [-\pi, \pi)$ that matches the data for $j = 0$ always exists if the total demand is bounded. This is true because for $j = 0$ the modes are of the form, $\exp(-n\omega i)$, and if we let the weighting function be

$(2\pi)^{-\frac{1}{2}}L(\omega)$ then the matching condition, $Q_{0,n} = \frac{1}{\sqrt{2\pi}} \int\limits_{-\pi}^{\pi} L(\omega)e^{-n\omega i}\,d\omega$, can

be recognized as the formula for the coefficients of the Fourier series expansion of $L(\omega)$. Hence, $L(\omega) = \frac{1}{\sqrt{2\pi}}\sum\limits_{m} Q_{0m}e^{m\omega i}$, and the particular solu-

tion corresponding to some data is $Q_{j,n} = \frac{1}{\sqrt{2\pi}} \int\limits_{-\pi}^{\pi} L(\omega)\xi(\omega)^j\,e^{-n\omega i}\,d\omega$.

This expression is uniformly bounded for all j if and only if the modulus of

$\xi(\omega)$ never exceeds 1. (The bound is $\frac{1}{\sqrt{2\pi}} \int\limits_{-\pi}^{\pi}|L(\omega)|d\omega$.) This is Von Neu-

mann's stability test.

The test is implemented by inserting the modes, $Q_{jn} = \xi(\omega)^j \exp(-n\omega i)$, into (4.6), solving for $\xi(\omega)$,

$$\xi(\omega) = \sum\limits_{l=-A}^{\infty} \beta_l \exp(l\omega i) / [1-\alpha\exp(\omega i)], \qquad (4.8)$$

and then checking that $|\xi(\omega)| \le 1$. The condition reduces to:

$$\left| \sum_{l=-A}^{\infty} \beta_l \exp(l\omega i) \right| \le |1 - \alpha\exp(\omega i)|; \quad \forall \omega \quad \text{(for stability.)} \quad \blacksquare \qquad (4.9)$$

Note too that if a system is stable we expect to find that $Q_{j,n} = 0$ for $j \to \infty$, since our data are finite and must decay. We now show that the rate of decay as j increases for a given n is linked to the second derivative of $\xi(\omega)$ for $\omega = 0$, which we denote ξ''. (Consideration of (4.8) shows that this derivative is a negative real number for proper, stable policies.) Now, to prove our assertion note from (4.7) and (4.8) that if the policy is proper then $\xi(0) = 1$. Furthermore, if the system is stable, i.e. $|\xi(\omega)| \le 1$, then the point $\omega = 0$ is a global maximum of $|\xi(\omega)|$, since $|\xi(0)| = 1$. If (as is usual) this maximum is unique, then for large j the integrand in the expression for $Q_{j,n}$ is negligible, except for values of ω close to 0. In this neighborhood, everything on the integrand is approximately constant, except for $\xi(\omega)^j$ which is approximated by $(1 + \frac{1}{2}\omega^2\xi'')^j \approx \exp(\frac{1}{2}j\xi''\omega^2)$; i.e., by a Gaussian bell curve. Thus, the integral for $Q_{j,n}$ can be evaluated by integrating the Gaussian expression in a fixed neighborhood of $\omega = 0$, and multiplying the result by the relevant constants. The final expression is proportional to $(-j\xi'')^{-\frac{1}{2}}$. This confirms that $Q_{j,n}$ tends to zero, and that it does so at a rate determined by $|\xi''|$. Therefore, as claimed, large $|\xi''|$ imply fast decay and high stability.

The expression for $Q_{j,n}$ also shows that if the largest modulus of $\xi(\omega)$ exceeds 1, $|\xi^*| > 1$, and this is achieved for a single value, ω^*, then the asymptotic solution for large j is determined by $|\xi^*|$ and ω^* alone. Thus, independently of the input data, the asymptotic solution should be oscillatory with a period of $2\pi/\omega^*$ intervals, and an amplitude that grows by an amplification factor $|\xi^*|$ with each step up the supply chain.

Multi-level systems can be treated in the same way, leading to a set of equations analogous to (4.6). The only difference in the result is that the right side of the equations must now include an extra set of terms, with sub-indices, $j-2,\ldots j-r$, for each additional supplier level considered by supplier j. The system of equations continues to be linear and homogeneous, and therefore amenable to Von Neumann's test. Of course, this is only meaningful when the number of links in the chain is greater than the number of levels, $J > r$.

4.3 Interpretation and examples

Equation (4.9) is a test for stability in the small. This is true because the uniform bound for $\{Q_{j,n}\}$ when (4.9) holds, $\frac{1}{\sqrt{2\pi}}\int_{-\pi}^{\pi}|L(\omega)|d\omega$, is itself bounded by the product of the maximum input deviation, δ', and the number of non-negative input values, N^+.[3] Hence, if (4.9) holds then the output bound is no greater than N^+ times the input bound; i.e., (4.1) holds with δ' = δ/N^+. If (4.9) is a strict inequality for all $\omega \neq 0$, the Von Neumann test implies something stronger than (4.1). In this case the amplitude of all modes tends to zero as $j \to \infty$ and, as a result, $\{Q_{jn} - Q\}$ tends to zero uniformly for all n.

Recall now that for linear systems the above analysis also holds for the order sizes and the inventory sequences themselves (of any size), and not just for small deviations from a steady state. Therefore, in the linear case, (4.9) is also a test for stability in the large. Hence, in the linear case the two forms of stability are equivalent, as shown in Fig. 4.1b, and failure of the test implies the bullwhip effect.

Simplified stability tests: A sufficient condition for stability, simpler but stricter than (4.9), is

$$\alpha, \ \beta_l \ \geq \ 0, \quad \text{for all } l \quad \text{(sufficient condition for stability.)} \quad (4.10)$$

This assumes that the policy is proper and (4.7) holds. That (4.7) and (4.10) imply (4.7) and (4.9) should be clear because if all the coefficients in (4.9) are non-negative, the left side of (4.9) is bounded from above by the sum of the β's and the left side is bounded from below by $1-\alpha$. Since (4.7) holds, the following must be true for all ω:

$$\left| \sum_{l=-A}^{\infty} \beta_l \exp(l\omega i) \right| \leq \sum_{l=-A}^{\infty} \beta_l = 1 - \alpha \leq \left| 1 - \alpha\exp(\omega i) \right|.$$

We now explore the relationship between gain, anticipation and stability. It will be argued, as illustrated in Fig. 4.1, that historical policies with

---

[3] To see this, simply note from the definition of $L(\omega)$ that $|L(\omega)| \leq N^+\delta'(2\pi)^{-\frac{1}{2}}$, and then integrate both sides of this inequality for $\omega \in [-\pi, \pi]$.

positive gains cannot be stable. To do this, an expression for the dimensionless gain in terms of the α- and β-coefficients is first derived.

Gain: Consider first the linear case, where (4.5) holds. Since (4.7) also holds, the expression $[N_{j-1,n+1} = \alpha N_{j-1,n+1} + \beta_{-A} N_{j-1,n+1} + \beta_{1-A} N_{j-1,n+1} + ..]$ is an identity that can be subtracted from (4.5). The difference of the two expressions relates the inventory of supplier j to the order rates of supplier $j-1$. In the steady state the result becomes $[K = \gamma + \alpha(K-Q) + \beta_{-A} (A-1)Q + \beta_{1-A}(A-2)Q + ...]$, from which we obtain the κ-function by solving for K. We find:

$$K = [\gamma - Q(\alpha + \sum_{l=-A}^{\infty} (l+1)\beta_l)]/(1-\alpha)$$

$$= [\gamma - Q(1 + \sum_{l=-A}^{\infty} l\beta_l)]/(1-\alpha). \qquad (\kappa\text{-function}) \qquad (4.11a)$$

Clearly the discrete gain is:

$$G = -(1 + \sum_{l=-A}^{\infty} l\beta_l)/(1-\alpha). \qquad (4.11b)$$

Since the gain of a non-linear system describes conditions that are nearly steady, where (2.13) can be approximated by (4.5), we see that (4.11b) also holds in the non-linear case. The significance of (4.7), (4.9) and (4.11b) is now explored with the help of some examples.

Example 4.3 (Forecasting with moving averages): We examine here adaptive policies where orders are determined with a moving average rule over $B > 0$ prior periods. This situation arises if the orders are based on forecasts, and the forecasts are based on historical averages. Policies of this type have an N-kernel with a single argument, $(N_{j-1,n} - N_{j-1,n-B})$ for some $B > 0$. Thus, linearized versions of any such policy can only have two non-zero coefficients, β_0 and β_B. Since these coefficients must add to unity they can be expressed as $\beta_0 = 1+\beta$ and $\beta_B = -\beta$, for some β. Thus, the linearized generic form of these policies has only one degree of freedom. Equation (2.9a) of Example 2.2 is the prototype.

Equations (4.11) can now be applied. They reveal, in agreement with (3.2b) and (3.4a), that the κ-function and gain are $\gamma + (\beta B-1)Q$ and $(\beta B-1)$, respectively. The gain is positive if $\beta \equiv \beta_0-1 > 1/B > 0$. This implies that

$\beta_0 > 1$ for positive gains, and that the two coefficients, β_0 and β_1, must have opposite signs. The complex amplitudes (4.8) are:

$$\xi(\omega) = \beta_0 + \beta_B \exp(B\omega i) \qquad\qquad (4.12a)$$

and we have

$$|\xi(\omega)|^2 = \xi(\omega)\,\overline{\xi(\omega)} = \beta_0^2 + \beta_B^2 + 2\beta_0\beta_B\cos(B\omega). \qquad\qquad (4.12b)$$

This expression is less than or equal to 1 for all ω if and only if β_0 and β_B have the same (positive) sign. The system is then stable, but has a negative gain. In this case, the rate at which disturbances are dissipated is $|\xi''| = \beta_B B^2$. Thus, we see that long averaging periods tend to stabilize the system.

If, on the other hand, β_0 and β_B have opposite signs, then $G > 0$, and the system is unstable. In this case, (4.12b) is maximized by $\omega^* = \pi/B$, and the amplification factor is: $|\xi^*| = |\beta_0| + |\beta_B| = 1 + 2|\beta_B| > 1$. ∎

Note that a complete oscillation would take $2(B\text{-}1)$ time periods. Since $|\beta_B| = (1+G)/(B-1)$, the disturbance growth rate can be reduced without changing the gain by increasing B. This would increase the period of the oscillations. For systems where it is expensive to change the production rates, suppliers have an incentive to use a large B, and to adapt sluggishly to the demand by keeping inventories. In industries where orders are placed infrequently (e.g., on the order of months) Bh may be comparable with a year or even longer. Thus, the supply chain effects discussed here would induce oscillations with a period of multiple years. It is generally accepted that inventories are an important cause of business cycles. Our result suggests a specific mechanism consistent with experience--since the predicted oscillation cycles are comparable with those observed.

Note too that the periodic review, order-up-to-level (R, S) policy discussed as Example 2.1, which is the special case of the current example with $\beta = 0$ and $G = -1$, is stable.

Example 4.4 (Inventory-based policies):   Inventory-based policies have an N-kernel with a single argument, $(N_{j,n} - N_{j-1,n})$. Example 2.3 is the prototype of all such policies, after linearization. We see from (2.10a) that the only two coefficients different from zero in (4.5) should be α, and $\beta_0 = (1-\alpha)$. Condition (4.9) with $\omega = \pi$ reveals that α cannot be negative if the policy is to be stable, Likewise, consideration of the case with $\omega = 0$ reveals that α cannot exceed 1. Hence, stability requires $\alpha \in [0, 1]$. In this range, however, $G < 0$; see (3.4b). ∎

Example 4.3 showed that all non-anticipative, order-based policies based on moving averages are unstable if $G > 0$. Example 4.4 obtained the same result for inventory-based policies; i.e., in this case too, a positive gain without anticipation implies instability. It turns out that this property of gain is generally true. The easiest way to see this is with the following qualitative and non-rigorous argument.

Consider first the order-based version of (4.6) with the following linear input: $Q_{0,n} = an$, if $n > 0$, and $Q_{0,n} = 0$, otherwise; see Fig. 4.2a. Recall that (4.6) applies to the deviations from a steady state for the order size. Therefore, the Q's in Fig. 4.2a can be positive or negative. With the given input, (4.6) predicts that the order deviations for supplier 1 should be $Q_{1,n+1} = an - a\Sigma_l \, l\beta_l$, for $n \geq B+1$. Therefore, if $\Sigma_l \, l\beta_l$ is negative then $|Q_{1,n+1}| > |Q_{0,n}| > |Q_{0,n-1}| \ldots$ for $n \geq B+1$. In other words, the output order size (deviation) always exceeds in absolute value the absolute value of the inputs used to determine it, as shown in Fig. 4.2a. This "positive feedback" effect is in force whether a is positive or negative. Since the effect also applies to $j = 2, 3, \ldots$ we see that it would be magnified with increasing j: output order sizes would be amplified along the supply chain when customer orders are increasing (positive a) or damped when they are decreasing (negative a). In terms of N-curves the result is as shown on Fig. 4.2b. Clearly, a policy with negative $\Sigma_l \, l\beta_l$ would increase the curvature of the N_j-curves with increasing j. Therefore, it is impossible for such a policy to dissipate all wiggles and return to a steady state.

Since the policies we are discussing are order-based ($\alpha = 0$), the condition $\Sigma_l \, l\beta_l \geq 0$ required for stability is equivalent to $G \geq -1$; see (4.11b). Therefore, we have just shown that $G + 1 \leq 0$ is a necessary condition for stability for non-anticipative, order-based policies. Similar arguments reveal that the result also holds for mixed policies. This justifies the claim of Fig. 4.1b, that the set $H^+ \cap S$ is empty.

In view of this, we should ask whether positive gains (which are desirable from the standpoint of individual suppliers) could be achieved without bad side effects by commitment-based, anticipative policies. A change of variable in the time coordinates can be used to reduce anticipative problems to the non-anticipative case, and thus, answer this question (in the positive). The mechanics of the procedure are explained in Sec. 5.2.2. The

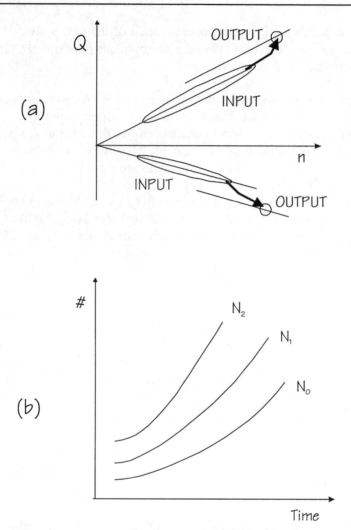

Figure 4.2. Performance of a linear, order-based strategy under steadily increasing demand

reader can verify with this method that the following condition is necessary for stability:

$$A \geq G+1 \qquad \text{(necessary condition for stability.)} \qquad (4.13)$$

This result is interesting because it links anticipation and gain: greater anticipation allows greater gains. An example is now provided.

Example 4.5 (Commitment-based policies): We revisit here the policies of Example 2.5.

For order-based policy (2.17a) all the coefficients are zero, except $\beta_{-A} = 1+\beta$ and $\beta_B = -\beta$. Thus, (4.7) is satisfied and the steady state exists. In terms of β, A and B, we find from (4.8) that $\xi(\omega) = (1+\beta)\exp(-A\omega i) - \beta\exp(B\omega i)$. Hence, $|\xi(\omega)|^2 = (1+\beta)^2 + \beta^2 - 2(1+\beta)\beta\cos((B+A)\omega) = 1 + 2(1+\beta)\beta[1-\cos((B+A)\omega)]$, and stability condition (4.9) can be expressed as:

$$|\xi(\omega)|^2 = 1 + 2(1+\beta)\beta[1-\cos((B+A)\omega)] \leq 1; \quad \forall\omega. \tag{4.14}$$

This condition is satisfied if and only if β and $1+\beta$ have different signs; i.e., if and only if $\beta \in [-1, 0]$.

To see how this condition is related to the gain, express β in terms of the gain. We know from (4.11b) or (3.4c) that $G = (A-1) + (A+B)\beta$. Hence, $\beta = (G+1-A)/(A+B)$, and we see that $\beta \in [-1, 0]$ if and only if $A \geq G+1$.

We also find after some manipulations that $\xi'' = \beta B^2 - (1+\beta)A^2 = (G+1)(B-A) - AB$, which declines with A. This means that the rate at which this policy smoothes out disturbances increases with A; i.e., that extra anticipation implies extra stability, as one would expect.

If the foregoing analysis is now repeated for policy (2.17b), we again find that the system is stable if and only if $A \geq G+1$, and that its stability increases with A. ∎

The futility of forecasting for positive gain: These results are important because, as we argue in the paragraph below, they establish that improvements in forecasting cannot eliminate instabilities if suppliers act on the forecasts so as to operate with a positive gain. Since positive gains are economical, this means that instability should be attacked in a different way than by improving the forecasts.

Let us now see why forecasting is not the issue. If a system was in a steady state and (perfect) forecasts were based on the order history of B periods, the forecasts would predict a continuation of the steady state. No other futures would be possible (!). Therefore, assuming that the future can be forecasted without error is tantamount to assuming away all but one of the future scenarios that can occur. This is not reasonable. However, if one allows forecasting errors of some size (possibly very small) then one must also allow for (small) deviations from a steady state. If such deviations are possible, even if they are very small, then the arguments in this section apply, and we must conclude that the set $H^+ \cap S$ is empty. Thus, history-based forecasting methods cannot be stable if suppliers insist on positive gains. We will see in Chapter 5 that this is also true for semi-autonomous chains where suppliers share information across levels.

On the other hand, all the comments about forecasting made in these notes pertain to "endogenous" forecasts, i.e., to predictions based on data previously generated by the policy. Thus, the logic behind the "impossibility" result does not apply to situations where an exogenous source of information (e.g., promises made by clients, or commitment contracts) can be used to make perfect predictions. Example 4.5 just showed that if these exogenous predictions have no error, then stable policies with a positive gain can be found. But if the exogenous information is subject to (small) errors, then instabilities will creep in again. (This is true because this situation corresponds to an endogenous system in which orders can deviate from the steady state within a small unpredictable band.) Thus, exogenous predictions (or commitments) with an anticipation value satisfying (4.13) are needed to stabilize a chain.

We will see in Sec. 4.4, below, that in addition to instabilities, order-based algorithms that violate (4.13) generate order cancellations. Thus, a violation of (4.13) also creates other pernicious effects. On the other hand, Chapter 5 will show that there are mixed algorithms that satisfy (4.13) as an equality and work well (i.e., are strongly stable, reliable and have no cancellations), even in the non-linear case.[4] Thus, the least possible anticipation for a properly working chain with gain G is $A = G+1$. Hence, any chain with gains G at all steps needs the following commitment horizon; see (2.16):

Required commitment horizon for gain $G = h[JG+1]$ (4.15)

Other necessary conditions: Equation (4.13) is not the only simple, necessary, stability condition that can be developed. Additional conditions can be obtained by examining specific properties of $\xi(\omega)$. For example, since, as we have already seen, $|\xi(\omega)|$ should have a global maximum at

---

[4] We already know how to do much of this for the linear case. In particular, note that the policies of Example 4.5 (with $A \geq G+1$) are strongly stable because they pass Von Neumann's test, and are linear. By adjusting their parameters γ, A, B and β (or γ, A and α) one can obtain a policy with any desired linear K-function; i.e., any desired steady state behavior. Thus, we only have to check if they are reliable and monotone.

$\omega = 0$, a simple test consists of checking whether it has a *local* maximum at $\omega = 0$ by examining its derivatives.

Another very simple condition can be obtained by taking averages in (4.9). This is justified because (4.9) holds for every ω. The result of taking averages is:

$$\alpha^2 + \Sigma_l \beta_l^2 \le 1 \quad \text{(necessary condition for stability.)} \quad (4.16)$$

This condition applies both to commitment-based (anticipative) and non-anticipative policies. This chapter is now ended with brief discussions of monotonicity, and queuing (or "push") systems.

4.4 Some additional properties of linear, order-based policies

In this section we restrict our attention to linear, order-based policies. It will be shown that monotonicity and stability are related, and that (4.13) is a necessary condition for monotonicity. We will find that monotonicity implies stability. Thus, for order-based policies, lack of stability implies order cancellations. We will also find conditions under which linear, order-based policies are reliable.[5]

Proposition 4.1 (Monotonicity of linear, order-based policies): A linear, order-based policy is monotonic if and only if all its β-coefficients are non-negative. ■

Proof: The proposition pertains to the exact instances of (4.6) where $\alpha = 0$. First, note from (4.6) that if the β-coefficients are non-negative, the expression will produce non-negative outputs for non-negative inputs (monotonicity). Thus, sufficiency is established, and we only need to show necessity; i.e., that monotonicity implies non-negativity of the coefficients. To do this, it suffices to show that if there is one negative coefficient, then negative orders can occur. This should be clear, however, because if the customer order sequence consists of a single impulse, i.e., $Q_{0,n} = 1$ if $n = n'$ and $Q_{0,n} = 0$ otherwise, then the output of (4.6) will be negative whenever the impulse coincides with a negative coefficient. ■

---

[5] Properly modified, the reliability arguments in this section can also be used with non-linear, mixed policies, at least in some cases. This is done in Sec. 5.2.4.

Consideration of this proposition shows that proper monotone policies satisfy (4.10). Therefore, they are stable.

It is also interesting to calculate the maximum gain that can be achieved with a monotone, order-based, policy. This question can be cast as the following linear programming problem, which relies on (4.11b) for the objective function, and on (4.7) and the proposition for the constraints:

$$ max \left\{ G = -1 - \sum_{l=-A}^{\infty} l\beta_l : \sum_{l=-A}^{\infty} \beta_l = 1 ; \quad \beta_l \geq 0, \ \forall l \right\}. $$

The optimum solution is obtained by setting the coefficient with the smallest sub-index equal to 1 ($\beta_{-A} = 1$) and all others equal to zero. This yields again the familiar result, $G = A - 1$. Thus, we see that (4.13) is also a necessary condition for monotonicity. Note that this necessary condition also applies to non-linear policies, since these policies behave linearly when the input is nearly steady.

Let us now turn our attention to reliability. Up to this moment the properties of our policies have been exclusively determined by their α- and β-coefficients. The inhomogeneous constant, γ, of (4.5) played no role. This was to be expected because this constant simply defines a vertical translation in the N-curves without influencing their wiggles. The reliability condition, however, is about separations between N-curves and must involve the constant. For strongly stable policies (with bounded order sizes and inventories), the maximum absolute separation between curves is obviously bounded. Therefore, in this case there must be a sufficiently large γ that guarantees reliability. An expression for the smallest γ that accomplishes this feat in the linear, order-based case is derived below. To do this, the following result is established first:

Proposition 4.2 (Order bounds of linear, order-based policies): If the β-coefficients of a linear, order-based policy are non-negative and satisfy $\Sigma_l \beta_l = 1$, and if the customer orders satisfy $Q_{0,n} \in [0, Q_{max}]$, then $Q_{j,n} \in [0, Q_{max}]$. ∎

Proof: Since such policies are monotone (Proposition 4.1), it suffices to show that $Q_{j,n+1} \leq Q_{j-1,max}$, where $Q_{j-1,max} = sup_n\{Q_{j-1,n}\}$. This is true, however, because $Q_{j,n+1} = \Sigma_l \beta_l Q_{j-1,n-l} \leq \Sigma_l \beta_l Q_{j-1,max} = Q_{j-1,max}$. ∎

We are now ready to present the following reliability test:

Proposition 4.3 (Reliability): If the β-coefficients of a linear, order-based policy are non-negative, and satisfy $\Sigma_l\,\beta_l = 1$, and if the customer orders satisfy $Q_{0,n} \in [0, Q_{max}]$, then the policy is reliable if $\gamma \geq \gamma_{min}$, where $\gamma_{min} = \Sigma_l\,\beta_l\,max\{0,(m+1+l)\}Q_{max}$. ∎

Proof: According to (1.5), we need to show that $N_{j,n+1} \geq N_{j-1,n+m+1}$ for all j and n, where $m = \lceil M/h \rceil$, if γ is within the specified range. Inserting (4.5) in the left side of this inequality, we find the equivalent condition for reliability:

$$\gamma + \Sigma_l\,\beta_l N_{j-1,n-l} \geq N_{j-1,n+m+1},$$

where the summation ranges from $-A$ to ∞, but includes only a finite number of non-zero β's. Since $\Sigma_l\,\beta_l = 1$, the reliability condition may be rewritten as

$$\gamma \geq \Sigma_l\,\beta_l[N_{j-1,n+m+1} - N_{j-1,n-l}].$$

Proposition 4.2 allows us to bound the factor in brackets by:

$$max\{0, (m+1+l)Q_{max}\} \geq [N_{j-1,n+m+1} - N_{j-1,n-l}].$$

Therefore, we can write:

$$\gamma_{min} \equiv \Sigma_l\,\beta_l\,max\{0,(m+1+l)\}Q_{max.} \geq \Sigma_l\,\beta_l[N_{j-1,n+m+1} - N_{j-1,n-l}] ,$$

where γ_{min} is a finite quality since the summation includes only a finite number of non-zero terms. Obviously then, the reliability condition must hold if $\gamma \geq \gamma_{min}$, as claimed. ∎

Note from its expression that the ideal value $\gamma_{min} = 0$ can only be attained by setting $\beta_l = 0$ for all $l \geq -m$; i.e., if positive coefficients are only used for terms with an anticipation greater than m ($l < -m$). This occurs for example in the special case of (2.17a) with $\gamma = \beta = 0$ and $A = m + 1$, which corresponds to "just-in-time" operations. The gain in this case is $G = A-1$ $= m$; see (3.4c). Greater gains can be achieved with the same policy by setting $A > m +1$. Smaller gains, however, require $\gamma_{min} > 0$.

We have not examined in this section the monotonicity and reliability properties of mixed policies, nor have we examined the stability-in-the-large properties of non-linear policies. These issues should be examined on a case by case basis, perhaps using similar logic. This is done in Section 5.2.4 for the "ACT" policy which is the focus of Chapter 5.

4.5 Duality: Serial queues and "push chains"

Recall from the discussion of Equations (2.18) and (2.19) in Section 2.5 that the equations of a queuing system are obtained by interchanging j and j-1 in the equations of the autonomous chain. If we do this for (2.13) and then linearize it, the general result is of the form:

$$N_{j-1,n+1} = \gamma' + aN_{j-1,n} + b_{-A}N_{j,n+A} + b_{1-A}N_{j,n+A-1} + \ldots \quad (n \text{ integer}; j = 1,\ldots J) \quad (4.17a)$$

Taking first forward differences in the above, we find,

$$Q_{j-1,n+1} = aQ_{j-1,n} + b_{-A}Q_{j,n+A} + b_{1-A}Q_{j,n+A-1} + \ldots \quad (n \text{ integer}; j = 1,\ldots J) \quad (4.17b)$$

These equations correspond to a stencil that is a mirror image of the pull-stencil shown in Fig. 2.2b.

Interchanging j and $j-1$ is the same as reversing the sign of the supplier number variable. Therefore, the solution of (4.17a) is the same as the solution of (4.5) after changing the sign of j and replacing the vector of coefficients (a, b) for (α, β). This means that the existence condition (4.7) continues to hold. The sign reversal in supplier number, however, changes inventories into "negative" queues. Thus, the expression for gain (4.11b) now holds with the sign reversed. Furthermore, if we express the modes of (4.17b) as $X(\omega)^{-j} \exp(-n\omega i)$ (note the changed sign of j), then $X(\omega)$ obeys the same expression as $\xi(\omega)$; namely:

$$X(\omega) = \sum_{l=-A}^{\infty} b_l \exp(l\omega i) / [1 - a\exp(\omega i)]. \quad (4.18)$$

For a series of queues to be stable, disturbances should not grow in the direction of decreasing j; i.e., the modulus of $X(\omega)$, rather than that of $\xi(\omega)$, should be bounded. Hence, the stability condition is the same as before:

$$\sup |X(\omega)| \le 1 \qquad (\text{stability in the direction of decreasing } j).$$

These observations show that if we define the dual of a policy with coefficients (α, β) to be a (queuing) policy with a mirror image stencil and coefficients $(a, b) = (\alpha, \beta)$, then both will be stable or unstable and their gains will be of the same magnitude but opposite sign.[6]

This relationship allows us to interpret condition (4.13) in an interesting way for queueing systems. If we let $G_q = -Q$ be the gain of a dual (queueing) policy, then (4.13) becomes $A \geq -G_q + 1$. Thus, a necessary stability condition for the usual type of queuing systems (where $A = 0$) is $G_q \geq 1$. In continuous time, this is $g_q \equiv G_q h \geq h$, which becomes $g_q > 0$ for $h \to 0$. Thus, queuing gains should be positive for stability. This indicates, in agreement with intuition, that queuing systems can be stable only if their service rate is an increasing function of queue length.

The duality results also show that stable queuing policies with positive gains exist, since stable, non-anticipative inventory management strategies with negative gains exist. This suggests another way in which a supply chain could be managed.

Push chains: In this (hypothetical) form of operation the upstream supplier J chooses freely its shipment sequence, with the ultimate goal of satisfying the customer demand. This supplier keeps J-1 informed of its shipping decisions by sending a "push-order" (or warning) of shipments to come, perhaps with some anticipation. Suppliers $J = 1, 2\ldots J$-1 operate with a queuing stencil, basing their decisions on the history of the number of items received, the number of committed orders, and the current number of orders/items in "queue". Supplier j also places a "push-order" (a warning of items coming to supplier j-1) with every shipment. The cumulative number of orders is the N_j curve. Of course, these warnings materialize as physical arrivals at j-1 after a transportation time, and the ensuing arrival times determine the S_{j-1} curve. A complete theory can be formulated as in the "pull case," in terms of the N-curves alone. Clearly, the general form of the equation is still that of (2.13) and (2.15), but with j and $(j-1)$ reversed. Those equations must now be complemented by a reliability constraint ensuring that the flow of physical items can keep up with the flow of orders. Consideration shows that this constraint continues to be (1.5):

$$N_{j-1}(t+M_j) \leq N_j(t), \quad \text{(reliability condition for push chains.)} \quad (4.19)$$

To ensure that (4.19) is satisfied, policies should include inhomogeneous constants, γ', that are sufficiently large; e.g., as recommended in Proposition 4.3. We call systems operated in this way "push" chains be-

---

[6] The duality results also apply to multi-level chains, since every chain of a given level has an image of opposite type with a symmetric stencil and the same coefficients.

cause items are "pushed" toward the customer, rather than pulled by its orders. The approach has merit because, as was mentioned earlier, it can achieve positive gains without anticipation or instabilities. Unfortunately it is rarely used in practice, perhaps because orders have to flow in the reverse direction from money, which seems impractical for complex supply networks with many levels. For systems with small J, it may be possible to design politically feasible re-supply contracts that transfer the decision-making authority toward J. In the automobile industry automakers negotiate with their dealers and structure agreements so they can set their production schedules with a mixture of specific orders from their dealers, and their own educated guesses. The idea of "vendor-managed inventories" is also in the same spirit.

5. Strongly Stable Policies: The Act Method

Chapter 4 showed how to test algorithms for stability in the small and presented examples of stable and unstable (linear) algorithms. The chapter also discussed the monotonicity and reliability of linear order-based algorithms. However, it did not examine in detail the general (non-linear) case. To be useful, general policies should avoid negative orders, be reliable in the sense of (1.5), be strongly stable, and stay close to dynamic target inventory levels while tracking the customer demand. Designing useful policies is more an art than a science. In the next few sections we present the simplest policy we have been able to envision with all these properties.

A dynamic inventory target is a function that gives the desired (order) inventories for all suppliers at each moment in continuous time as a function of the customer input data (past and future), also in continuous time. Equivalently, it is a function that gives a set of continuous time N-curves, $u_j(t)$, for a given customer demand curve. Targets should have all the properties demanded of the policies that will track them (strong stability, monotonicity, etc) and be appealing to the suppliers from a cost-efficiency standpoint. Targets do not have to be step functions. They are useful because they are easy to construct, and they provide something to "shoot for." The choice of a target is an economic issue, and this will be explored in Chapter 6. Here, we will restrict our attention to the development of autonomous policies that can track all the targets in a broad family. Section 5.1, below, focuses on the targets and Sec. 5.2 on the policies.

5.1 The kinematic wave target

The targets proposed in these lecture notes are solutions of the kinematic wave (KW) model of fluids; see Lighthill and Whitham (1955), Richards (1956), Lax (1973) and Newell (1993) for background on this theory. The theory pertains to the flow of generic items such as fluid particles, cars or order acknowledgements over one-dimensional "pipes". Therefore, it is relevant to the supply chain problem if we just imagine that suppliers are located on a "pipe", spaced p distance units apart such that their distances from the customer are $x_j = jp$. The solution of a KW problem can be expressed by means of a bivariate function, $u(x, t)$, that gives the item number at every point in continuous space-time. As pointed out in Makigami et al (1971), this function contains all the information necessary to keep track of everything of importance. For example, the iso-u contours of the surface are curves in space-time that depict the trajectory of a specific order number:

$$u(x, t) = \#   \text{(trajectory of order number \#)} \tag{5.1}$$

A set of trajectories for closely spaced # give a "topographic" map of the solution; see Fig. 5.1a. The target curves, $u_j(t)$, can be retrieved from the solution by expressing the order number as a function of time at the locations of the suppliers: $u_j(t) = u(x_j, t)$. Fig. 5.1b depicts the target curves for the solution of Fig. 5.1a.

There are two reasons for adopting KW theory. First, as we explain below, the KW targets, $u_j(t)$, have all the desired properties mentioned above (monotonicity, reliability and strong stability). Second, since a discrete-time approximation theory to the KW model already exists, it can be used for policy development; this will be done in Sec. 5.2. The following is a brief primer on KW theory. It is divided into three parts: the problem, the solution, and its properties.[1]

The KW problem: A KW problem is specified by: (i) boundary data in the form of a smooth non-decreasing customer demand curve, $N_0(t) \equiv u_0(t)$, and (ii) a K-function. The KW solution must: (i) satisfy the boundary condition,

$$N_0(t) \equiv u_0(t) \equiv u(0, t), \tag{5.2}$$

(ii) have "inventory densities" that are everywhere consistent with the K-function and the "local order rate," and (iii) be "stable".

---

[1] A more detailed but less conventional introduction to KW theory is given in Appendix B.

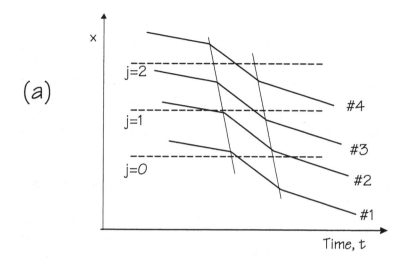

(a)

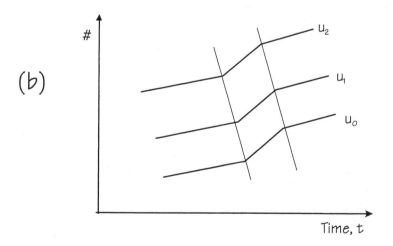

(b)

Figure 5.1. The kinematic wave target for a linear K-function : (a) item trajectories ; (b) target curves.

The second condition is expressed mathematically as the following equation for the u function:

$$\partial u/\partial x = K(\partial u/\partial t)/p. \tag{5.3}$$

The left side of (5.3) is the rate at which the item number increases with space. It will be called the inventory density, or "density," and denoted "ρ". The argument of the K-function in (5.3) is the rate at which u increases with time. It will be called the local order rate, or "flow," and denoted "f." In the steady state, ρ and f are constant, and (5.3) shows that they must satisfy $\rho p = K(f)$. This is consistent with the idea of a K-function since ρp is the number of orders between consecutive suppliers, i.e., the steady state target inventory.[2]

Although solutions satisfying (i) and (ii) always exist for problems with physically meaningful data, such solutions are not always unique for problems with non-linear K-functions. Condition (iii) restores uniqueness in the non-linear case by ruling out spurious solutions. We will return to this point towards the end of this section, when covering the solution properties; see also Appendix B.

The solution of (5.2) and (5.3): Equation (5.3) is a first order partial differential equation. Therefore, it should have solutions that satisfy (5.2) for all t. These solutions should satisfy (5.3) everywhere except, perhaps, at curves called "shocks" where the partial derivatives of the solution may have a jump discontinuity.

When the K-function is linear, $K = K_o + gf$, the solution is unique and does not require shocks if $u_0(t)$ is smooth. The solution is:

$$u(x, t) = u_0(t+xg/p) + xK_o/p. \tag{5.4}$$

The reader can verify that (5.4) satisfies (5.2) and (5.3) everywhere. Its uniqueness can be established with a variety of methods (e.g., the method of the Monge cones--see Garabedian, 1986).

---

[2] To avoid the proliferation of symbols, we have used "$K(\ )$" for the K-function of the target. This symbol has been used earlier for the K-function of the algorithm. Using a common symbol is reasonable because all algorithms considered here will turn out to have the same steady states as the target. Note, however, that we use f for the flow of the target at any given time instead of q (the actual flow) since the two flows will generally be different.

Consideration of (5.4) shows that the flow $f = \partial u/\partial t$ (and its temporal variations) propagate as "waves". This can be clearly seen by taking partial derivatives with respect to t in (5.4), which yields: $f(x,t) = f_o(t+xgp/p)$. Obviously, flow (and its derivatives) must be constant along any straight line of the form, $t+xg/p = t_o$, for any given t_o. Such lines are called wave trajectories. Note that both, f and its derivatives are always replicated at locations with different x with a time lag, as if transmitted by a wave. The wave velocity is $-p/g$. Alternatively, we say that the wave travels with a constant "pace" of $-g/p$ time units per unit distance.

Since the wave pace is the same for all waves, the set of all waves is a family of parallel lines; these are the thin solid lines shown in Fig. 5.1. Furthermore, since (5.3) is satisfied everywhere, we see that not only the flow but also the density is constant along each wave. Moreover, since the "speed" of an order, i.e., the slope of a trajectory in Fig. 5.1a, is given by dx/dt for constant # in (5.1), we see that it can be expressed as: $-(\partial u/\partial t)/(\partial u/\partial x) = -f/\rho$. Since the flow and density are constant along a wave, this shows that the "order speed" must also be constant along the wave. Hence, waves also transmit changes in order speed, as illustrated in Fig. 5.1a.[3]

Since order trajectories must have the same slope when they intersect the same wave, it follows that all order trajectories should be translationally symmetric in the direction of the wave trajectories; i.e., they must be parallel lines, as shown in Figure 5.1a. The target curves must also be parallel (see Fig. 5.1b). This can be seen by substituting jp for x in (5.4), which yields:

$$u_j(t) = u_0(t+jg) + jK_o \tag{5.5a}$$

or equivalently,

$$u_j(t) = u_{j-1}(t+g) + K_o. \tag{5.5b}$$

These equations are Newell's "up and over" rule (Newell, 1993) for constructing N-curves in linear KW problems. Finally note that in the steady state (with customer order rate q_0) the solution surface for linear problems is a plane:

$$u(x, t) = \text{constant} + q_0 t + x(K_o + q_0 g)/p \quad \text{(in the steady state.)} \tag{5.6}$$

---

[3] This is why these waves are called "kinematic" waves.

The reader can verify that in the non-linear case (5.6) is generalized by:

$$u(x, t) = \text{constant} + q_0 t + x K(q_0)/p \qquad \text{(in the steady state.)} \qquad (5.7)$$

The time-dependent solution for non-linear problems is not as easy to generalize. It is known, however, that the solution also includes waves, where the order flow, density and speed are constant. To see this, take the derivative with respect to time of (5.3) and substitute $(\partial\rho/\partial t)$ for $(\partial f/\partial x)$ on the left side (we can do this since the cross derivatives of u should be the same independent of the order in which they are taken). The result is:

$$\partial f/\partial x = [g(f)/p]\partial f/\partial t, \qquad (5.8)$$

where we have used g for the derivative of K. Consider now the differential of f along a straight line on the (t, x) plane with

$$dt/dx = -[g(f)/p] \qquad \text{(wave pace.)} \qquad (5.9)$$

Since $df=[\partial f/\partial x]dx+[\partial f/\partial t]dt$, we see from (5.8) and (5.9) that this differential vanishes, and that f is then constant along the line. These lines are called "characteristics" or "waves". Not only f but also ρ and the order speed are constant along a wave, as in the linear case. Equation (5.9) gives the pace with which this information is transmitted. Thus, the time lag between suppliers is:

$$\text{wave trip time from supplier } j-1 \text{ to } j = -g(f). \qquad (5.10)$$

Notice that in the non-linear case the wave pace is different across waves, since it depends on f. Thus, waves tend to focus or spread, and this is why complete solutions require the introduction of shocks. In the non-linear case, order trajectories are no longer parallel, either. However, they continue to adopt the pace "demanded" by the waves they encounter; i.e., the ratio $-\rho/f$. Since (5.3) states that $\rho = K(f)/p$ everywhere (except on shocks), it follows that the local order pace is:

$$\text{order pace} = -K(f)/pf. \qquad (5.11)$$

A physical consequence of the above mathematical facts is that all the differences in two solutions of a problem with identical input data except for an infinitesimal local perturbation in flow must be confined to the wave on the (x, t) plane that contains the perturbation. Thus, waves can be thought of the medium on which cause and effect are connected.

Finally note from (5.9) that if the local gain (g, with units of time) is positive the wave pace is negative; i.e., waves hit upstream suppliers first, as indicated by (5.10). This is graphically demonstrated by Fig. 5.2, where one can geometrically see the connection between gain and wave direction. Since a KW solution with positive g "anticipates" changes in flow by an amount (5.10), we see that the linkage between anticipation and gain surfaces again with continuous time targets. This observation will turn out to be important because, as is explained in Sec. 5.2, the character of the algorithms used to approximate the KW solution in discrete time is strongly influenced by wave behavior.

Properties of the KW solution: We show here that the KW solution is unique (in the sense explained below), continuous, monotonic, reliable and strongly stable.

Existence and uniqueness. We have already mentioned that the KW solution exists and is unique in the linear case. In the non-linear case, however, it is sometimes possible to find multiple solutions with different shock patterns. Fortunately, when this happens, there is always one and only one solution with "stable" shocks; i.e., such that if any shock was smoothed at any point in time then the shock would form again (rather than dissipate). Solutions without this property are only of mathematical interest since they could not physically arise; they would self-destruct.[4] The existence and uniqueness of a physically meaningful solution follows from the fact that methods for finding it always yield a unique result.[5] It is beyond the scope of this monograph to give an exhaustive discussion of solution methods, but one of these is included in Appendix B. From now on, when we talk about the KW solution, we will always mean the unique, physically meaningful solution of (5.2) and (5.3). It is in this sense that we can say that for any customer demand curve and any smooth but possibly non-linear K-function, there is a unique KW solution.

Continuity: We have already said that any solution of (5.3), $f(x, t)$, is smooth except for jump discontinuities at shocks. Therefore, $u(x, t)$ must be continuous.

---

[4] Mathematicians, e.g. Lax (1973), call this property the "entropy condition."

[5] A proof along different lines can be found in Lax (1973).

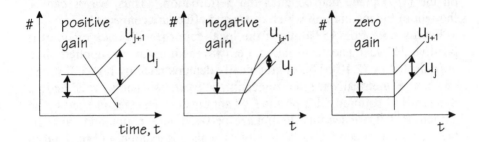

Figure 5.2. The relationship between gain and wave direction.

Monotonicity: All the solution methods, whether based on waves or successive (piecewise linear) approximations as in Appendix B, reveal that the least flow in the solution cannot be less than the least flow in the input data. Thus, if the input (customer data) contains no negative flows, the solutions cannot contain them either.

Reliability: Recall from the end of Chapter 3 that a K-function was said to be "reliable" if all its steady states were reliable as per (1.5); see Fig. 3.2b. This "curve-above-the-ray" property was a necessary condition for reliability, but it was not shown to be sufficient. Fortunately, it turns out that all KW solutions with reliable K-functions are reliable. To establish this, it suffices to show that all the target curves of a KW solution with a reliable K-function are always separated horizontally by at least M time units for all order numbers; i.e., that all the order number trip times exceed or equal M. We have seen, however, that the order pace is given by (5.10). Therefore, the trip time of an order for a distance $-p$ between consecutive suppliers is the product of this distance and the average of the (negative) paces experienced by the order along its trajectory, $p<K(f)/pf> = <K(f)/f>$. Since an average cannot be less than the least possible value of the quantities averaged, we can write $<K(f)/f> \geq inf(K(f)/f)$. And since $inf(K(f)/f) \geq M$ if the K-function is reliable (see Fig. 3.2b), it follows that any order trip time, $p<K(f)/pf>$, must exceed or equal M, as claimed.

Strong stability: It is shown in Daganzo (1997) that the KW solution satisfies an even more stringent condition than is required for strong stability; namely, that the maximum separation between pairs of consecutive KW target curves, $sup\{u_j(t)-u_{j-1}(t)\}$, is non-increasing in j. Because the proof of this statement is lengthy, it is relegated to Appendix B, which summarizes the relevant parts of this reference.[6] This result is very useful because it guarantees that the maximum target accumulation between suppliers is so tightly bounded that it cannot increase with j. Therefore, a discrete-time policy does not have to track a KW target very accurately to be strongly stable.

5.2 Discrete-time approximations of the KW target

Applied to some customer demand curve, a policy such as (2.1) or (2.2) generates data, N, on a space-time lattice that can be compared with a KW target, u. If the policy remains close to the target, it should share (at least approximately) the properties of the target. Closeness to a KW target is also useful because the long-run costs of policies with this property can be estimated easily. This will be explained in Chapter 6. The focus in this section is on their basic properties (stability, monotonicity and reliability). Section 5.2.1, below, gives some results that can be used to evaluate the tracking ability of arbitrary policies; section 5.2.2 proposes a very simple policy with good tracking properties; and sections 5.2.3 and 5.2.4 evaluate this policy in detail.

5.2.1 General Results for Linear Targets

The theory of numerical approximations to conservation laws (see LeVeque, 1992) can be used to evaluate tracking ability. This theory describes and evaluates recipes to approximate u at the points of a rectangular space-time lattice with intervals h (time) and p (distance). The recipes have the form of partial difference equations, of which our inventory control policies are special cases. Therefore, policies such as (2.13) can be evaluated with the theory.

A specific recipe is said to "converge" if its output, N, for a specific point in space-time converges to the true value of u, as the mesh spacings h and p tend to zero in a given ratio. Methods exist to evaluate the convergence rate and the order of the error, in terms of the mesh size. Because for supply chain problems operated with discrete-time policies the mesh size cannot be made as small as desired (it may be considered fixed for all practical purposes), "convergence" for these problems only means that the

---

[6] Because the treatment of KW theory in this reference is unconventional but tailor-made for inventory problems, readers familiar with KW theory may still want to scan the appendix.

tracking error tends to zero if the rate of variation of the customer orders also tends to zero; i.e., if the customer demand varies slowly with time.[7] The results do guarantee that if the demand rate stabilizes around a fixed value, then a discrete-time policy will stabilize all the supplier orders and inventories around those of the target. This is desirable. However, the error estimates about to be given should only be used as rough guides.

The disclaimer in the previous paragraph does not apply to flex-time policies, since in this case information technologies allow the review period to be shortened as much as desired without any economic impact.

In any case, for linear policies with mesh (h, p), there are two requirements for convergence: (i) the VonNeumann stability condition should be satisfied, and (ii) the "local truncation error" should be of order $o(h)$ as $h, p \rightarrow 0$ in a given ratio. The local truncation error is the difference between N and u at a generic point (x, t) when N is calculated with one iteration of the recursion, using as data the true values of u at the input ends of the stencil. For stable, linear models the global error is of the same order of magnitude with respect to (h, p) as the truncation error.

For the sake of illustration, let us now evaluate the truncation error of the general, linear autonomous policy, given by (4.5). Equation (4.5) yields

$$N_{j,n+1} = \gamma + \alpha u_{j,n} + \beta_{-A} u_{j-1,n+A} + \beta_{1-A} u_{j-1,n+A-1} + \dots \tag{5.12}$$

for the predicted value of N. According to (5.4), however, the true solution is of the form

$$u(x, t) = u_0(t+xg/p) + xK_o/p. \tag{5.13}$$

By expanding this expression in a power series about the point (x_j, t_{n+1}) we can express the inputs to (5.12) in terms of $u_{j,n+1} = u(x_j, t_{n+1})$, plus some deviations. Substituting these estimates in (5.12) will yield an expression for $N_{j,n+1}$ that reveals its difference with $u_{j,n+1}$.

Note from (5.13) that the first partial derivatives of $u(x, t)$ with respect to x and t are, respectively, $(g/p)f + K_o/p$ and f, where f is the first derivative of u_0. If we use f' for the second derivative of u_0, then the second partial derivatives of u with respect to xx, xt and tt are $(g/p)^2 f'$, $(g/p)f'$ and

---

[7] This is true because the fractional error of a policy cannot depend on the scale of measurement; i.e., the error cannot change if we gradually change the scales for time and space as p and h are reduced so as to leave their numerical values unchanged. The change of scale does smooth out the numerical input values, however, and this is why errors should tend to zero if the rate of variation tends to zero.

f', respectively. With this notation, and ignoring terms of third and higher order in h and p, we find after a few manipulations that:

$$N_{j,\,n+1} \cong [\gamma - K_o \Sigma \beta_l] + u_{j,n+1}[\alpha + \Sigma \beta_l] - fh[(1+g/h)\Sigma \beta_l + \Sigma l \beta_l + \alpha] +$$

$$+ \tfrac{1}{2} f' h^2 [\alpha + \Sigma \beta_l (l+1+g/h)^2], \tag{5.14}$$

where the summations extend from $-A$ to infinity. Equation (5.14) shows that the truncation error, $N_{j,\,n+1} - u_{j,n+1}$, is of order $o(h)$ if

$$\gamma = K_o \Sigma \beta_l, \quad [\alpha + \Sigma \beta_l] = 1 \quad \text{and} \quad [(1+g/h)\Sigma \beta_l + \Sigma l \beta_l + \alpha] = 0. \tag{5.15}$$

The second equality in (5.15) merely restates existence condition (4.7). Consideration also shows that the third equality matches (4.11b); i.e., that this equality is satisfied if and only if the gain of the policy matches the gain of the target. Therefore, the truncation error is of first order or better if the policy is proper, has the same gain as the target, and we choose $\gamma = K_o \Sigma \beta_l$. Convergence to the KW target is assured if the policy also satisfies (4.9). Thus, we see that the conditions for existence, gain and stability found in Chapter 4, are intimately related to those of convergence. The magnitude of the truncation error can be evaluated from the last term of (5.14) and this is shown by means of two examples.

Example 5.1 (Accuracy of linear, order-based policies): Assume that $\alpha = 0$, $\Sigma \beta_l = 1$, and that all the β's are non-negative. We saw in Sec. 4.4 that this class of policies is monotone, and stable. Assume too that $\gamma = K_o$ and $\Sigma l \beta_l = -(1+g/h) \equiv -(1+G)$, so that (5.15) is satisfied. Then, the policy should track any KW target with gain g with first order precision, or better.

Note that the set of coefficients $\{\beta_l\}$ has all the properties of a probability distribution with mean $-(1+g/h) \equiv -(1+G)$, and that the factor in brackets in the last term of (5.14) is the variance of $\{\beta_l\}$. This shows that smaller errors are associated with smaller variances, and that the most accurate algorithms are those where the weights $\{\beta_l\}$ are concentrated around a single value. In fact, the most precise algorithm is obtained if we choose $\beta_{-(1+G)} = 1$. The policy in question is:

$$N_{j,n+1} = K_o + N_{j-1,n+G+1}, \tag{5.16}$$

which coincides with (2.20a). This algorithm is exact, because if (5.16) is iterated j times (and we reduce the time index by 1 on both sides of the resulting equality) we find:

$$N_{j,n} = jK_o + N_{0,n+jG} , \tag{5.17}$$

which matches (5.5a) precisely. ∎

Example 5.2 (Accuracy of linear, inventory-based policies): The general, stable linear inventory-based policy was discussed in Examples 2.3 and 4.2. Recall that its coefficients are zero, except for γ, $\alpha \in [0, 1]$ and $\beta_0 = 1-\alpha$. According to (3.4b), its gain is $G = -1/(1-\alpha)$ which for the allowed values of α, satisfies $G \leq -1$. Therefore, if we wish to track a KW target with parameters K_o and g we should set $\gamma = K_0$ and $-1/(1-\alpha) \equiv G = g/h$, so that (5.15) holds. The policy will then track the target with at least first order precision.

The factor in brackets in the last term in (5.14) is now $\alpha + (1-\alpha)(1+G)^2 = \alpha/(1-\alpha) = -(1+G) = -(1+ g/h)$. Thus, the policy is most accurate when g/h is close to -1. If $g/h = -1$, the policy coincides with (5.16) and is exact. If $g/h > -1$, however, the policy is unstable. ∎

It is interesting to note from these examples that the coefficient of f' in the last term of (5.14) is non-negative. Since $N_{j,n+1} \cong u_{j,n+1} + \frac{1}{2}f'h^2[\alpha+\Sigma\beta_i(l+1+g/h)^2]$, this means that wherever $f' > 0$ (i.e., u is convex with time) the policy tends to overshoot the target. As a result, the curvature of N should be less than the curvature of u if $f' > 0$. Consideration shows that the policy also reduces curvature (by undershooting the target) if $f' < 0$. This is typical of all stable policies. The effect tends to smooth out wiggles in demand, and the higher the truncation error the higher the smoothing effect.

Non-linear targets/policies can be studied similarly. One would first look for non-linear policies that behave as described above when the input data only includes small deviations from a steady state (so that linearization is possible), but then one would also have to check with ad-hoc methods that a candidate policy has all the required properties for large deviations. The following two subsections demonstrate this approach by first developing a family of policies that can track any non-linear KW target, and then showing that the family has all the required properties.

5.2.2 The ACT family

Inventory-based policies turn out to be the simplest. The general non-anticipative form of these policies is derived from the discrete-time version of (5.3), $K_{j,n} = K(Q_{j,n}/h)$; i.e.:

$$Q_{j,n} = hK^{-1}(K_{j,n}) \qquad \Leftrightarrow \qquad N_{j,n+1} = N_{j,n} + hK^{-1}(K_{j,n}), \qquad (5.18)$$

where K is for the moment assumed to have an inverse. Equation (5.18) is an "upwind" differencing scheme for scalar conservation laws; see LeVeque (1992). A generalization of this method for systems of equations, called the "cell-transmission" (CT) algorithm, has been proposed for multi-commodity traffic networks (Daganzo, 1994). Since our ultimate goal in these lecture notes is extending the results about to be developed to multi-commodity freight networks, the name "cell-transmission" will be used for rule (5.18). For the CT recipe to be a valid approximation, however, it has to satisfy the following condition.

Courant's stability condition: Recall that waves are the medium on which cause and effect are connected; i.e., that the true value of f at any given point in space-time (x_a, t_a) cannot be affected by data on points that are not on a wave path passing through the point in question. In other words, the wave passing through (x_a, t_a) is the set of points, $D(x_a, t_a)$, whose data may influence $f(x_a, t_a)$. This set of points is called the "domain of dependence" of point (x_a, t_a). The domain of dependence for a numerical approximation such as (5.18), D_A, is defined similarly; i.e., so that data from points (x, t) not in D_A cannot affect $Q(x_a, t_a)$, regardless of the discretization used. The shadowed wedge in Fig. 5.3a is D_A for the point at the vertex and a numerical algorithm with the shown stencil. Other stencils would have different domains of dependence; see Figs. 5.3b and 5.3c. It should be clear that if data are defined on a region B of the (t, x)-plane and we find that $B \cap D(x_a, t_a) \not\subset B \cap D_A(x_a, t_a)$, then one could vary the initial data in the parts of D not included in D_A so as to change $f(x_a, t_a)$ without having an effect on $Q(x_a, t_a)$. Thus, the finite difference approximation could not approximate the target. The problem can be seen to arise in Figs. 5.3a and 5.3b but not in Fig. 5.3c, for systems where the boundary would include the line $x = 0$. Courant's necessary condition for convergence states that the domain of dependence of an algorithm must include all possible waves. ∎

Figure 5.3a clearly shows that all historical (non-anticipative) algorithms fail Courant's condition if the gain is positive. This result applies to autonomous and non-autonomous algorithms, with stencils as complicated as one wishes; see Fig. 5.3b. Hence, supply chains without commitments cannot track KW targets with positive gain. This result is consistent with the comments made in Sec. 4.3 about the "futility" of forecasting.

Figure 5.3c shows that autonomous, anticipative policies will meet Courant's condition if D_A encloses the wave path when it is shallowest; i.e., when the gain is largest. Thus, the necessary condition is:

$$Ah \geq h + g_{max} \quad \Leftrightarrow \quad A \geq 1 + G_{max} , \tag{5.19}$$

where $g_{max} = sup(dK/df)$. This is consistent with our earlier findings, (4.13).

It is known that CT rule (5.18) converges to the KW target if and only if (5.19) is satisfied. Since the CT rule is non-anticipative ($A = 0$), its convergence condition is $g_{max} \leq -h$, or $G_{max} \leq -1$; i.e., it can only work with negative gains. Unfortunately, this is unsatisfactory for our purposes. A change of variable is used below to overcome this difficulty.

The change to asynchronous time and the ACT rule: The reader can verify that the KW problem defined by (5.2) and (5.3) is invariant under the following transformation to "asynchronous time," where c is a constant with units of "pace" (time/distance):

$$t' = t + cx ; \quad x' = x ; \quad u' = u ; \quad and \ K'(f) = K(f) - cpf ; \tag{5.20a}$$

i.e., if for every distance unit, the clocks are advanced c time units and the K-function is redefined as shown in Figs. 5.4a and 5.4b. The transformation of the space-time domain is shown in Figs. 5.4c and 5.4d. Note that the discrete-time, $n = t/h$, is transformed as follows:

$$n' = n + (c/h)x = n + (cp/h)j, \tag{5.20b}$$

and that the supplier number is not affected by the transformation, i.e., $j' = j$. Invariance means that one can solve the problem in asynchronous time and then undo the transformation to obtain the desired solution. The transformation is useful because with a proper choice of c the transformed problem can be made to satisfy Courant's condition. Because the $\{n'\}$ must be integer, the choice of c must be such that the coefficient $(cp/h) \equiv A$ of (5.20b) is also an integer.

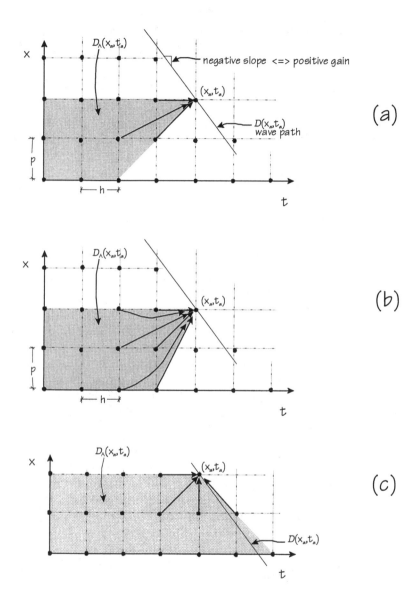

Figure 5.3. Domains of dependence for different policies: (a) autonomous, historical; (b) 2-level, historical; (c) autonomous, commitment-based

To see how Courant's condition constrains our choice of c (or A), note that the transformed maximum gain, $g'_{max} = sup(dK'/df) = sup(dK/df) - cp = g_{max} - cp$, can be made as small as needed as long as $g_{max} \neq \infty$ by increasing c. Thus, the CT convergence criterion, $g'_{max}/h \leq -1$, will be satisfied by choosing $A \equiv cp/h \geq 1 + g_{max}/h$. It follows that the following version of (5.18) converges:

$$Q_{j,n'} = hK'^{-1}(N_{j,n'} - N_{j-1,n'}), \tag{5.21}$$

where $n' = n + Aj$, and $A \equiv cp/h$ as per (5.20b). Note that K' is monotone-decreasing and will have an inverse, even if K does not. In original time, policy (5.21) becomes:

$$Q_{j,n} = hK'^{-1}(N_{j,n} - N_{j-1,n+A}), \text{ with } K'(f) = K(f) - Ahf; A \geq 1 + g_{max}/h. \tag{5.22a}$$

This is the proposed "asynchronous cell-transmission" (ACT) rule. In terms of the N-curves alone, the rule is:

$$N_{j,n+1} = N_{j,n} + hK'^{-1}(N_{j,n} - N_{j-1,n+A}), \text{ with } K'(f) = K(f) - Ahf; A \geq 1 + g_{max}/h \tag{5.22b}$$

∎

Note that with this rule, orders placed by j are just a function of $N_{j,n} - N_{j-1,n+A}$. We call this quantity, which can be positive or negative, the "*asynchronous order inventory*" (or "*asynchronous inventory*" for short) because it is the order inventory of j in the transformed time coordinates. In original coordinates, the asynchronous inventory is the current order inventory minus the future orders to which $j-1$ has already committed. Thus, the ACT algorithm is neither inventory-based nor order-based, but mixed.

Note that the mixed policy (2.17c) of Example 2.6 is just a linear version of the ACT policy. Since we found in Example 4.5 that the policy of Example 2.6 was stable-in-the-small if it satisfied $A \geq G + 1$, as required in (5.22a), it follows that the ACT policy must be stable-in-the-small too. Other properties of the ACT policy are explored in sections 5.2.3 and 5.2.4.

The ACT algorithm is so easy to implement that simulations can be done with spreadsheets. Figure 5.5 depicts some results for a case with seven suppliers. Part (a) is the result obtained for a linear K-function with positive gain, $g = h$ ($G = 1$). Note the closeness of the curves, and the absence of increased separations with increased j. Parts (b) to (d) depict nonlinear results with a concave-increasing K-function. Part (b) uses the same customer data as part (a), but it was obtained by setting $A = g_{max}/h$, which violates stability condition (5.19). Note how the inventories become increasingly chaotic with increasing j. Part (c) repeats the simulation with the same customer data and the same K-function, but using instead $A = 1 + g_{max}/h$, which guarantees stability. The figure clearly shows that the separation between curves is bounded, and that the curves become smoother as j increases despite the appearance of sharp bends or "shocks" -- as predicted in KW theory. The same is observed (even more clearly) in part (d) of the figure, which repeats the simulation with noisier customer data and a higher demand rate. In both cases, (c) and (d), the inventory fluctuations can be seen to decline with increasing j. In fact, the maximum inventory held by a supplier actually decreases with j. In part (d), the maximum inventories from $j = 1$ to $j = 7$ were: 6.54, 5.96, 5.44, 5.31, 5.26, 5.23 and 5.23 units, respectively.

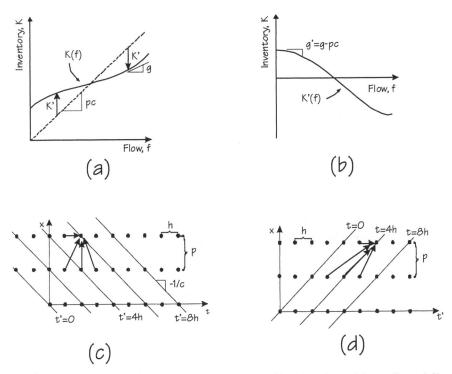

Figure 5.4. The transformation to asynchronous time: (a) K-functions; (b) transformed K-functions; (c) time-space domain; (d) transformed time-space domain.

As in the traffic flow case, the ACT procedure can also be used for in-homogeneous supply chains, where the K-functions depend on the supplier. The recursion is then:

$$Q_{j,n}= hK_j{}^{\prime-1}(N_{j,n}-N_{j-1,n+Aj}), \text{ with } K_j{}^{\prime}(f)=K_j(f)-A_jh \; ; A_j \geq 1+g_{j,max}/h. \quad (5.22c)$$

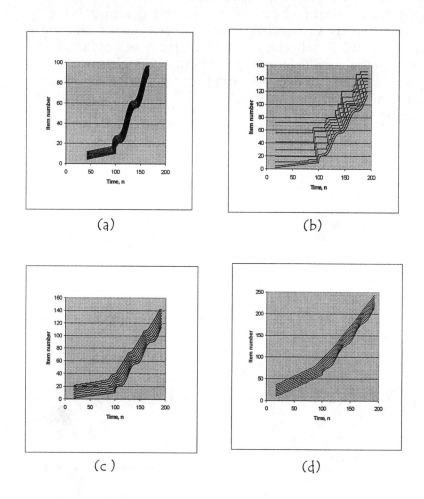

(a)

(b)

(c)

(d)

Figure 5.5. Cumulative N-curves for seven suppliers: (a) linear model with exact algorithm; (b) non-linear model with ACT algorithm, $cp - g_{max} = 0$ (unstable); (c) non-linear model with ACT algorithm, $cp - g_{max} = h$ (stable); (d) non-linear model with noisy data and ACT algorithm, $cp - g_{max} = h$ (stable).

Again, this indicates that the number of orders placed (acknowledgements received) by supplier j at time n is a function of the asynchronous order inventory of that supplier at time n. The next two sections examine the basic properties of the ACT policy. The linear case, because of its simplicity, is considered first.

5.2.3 Properties of the linear ACT policy: linear case and JIT systems

We show that the in linear case, the ACT policy with the least possible anticipation is, both, well behaved (monotone, reliable and strongly stable), and related to "just-in-time" (JIT) methods.

To see that the first part of this statement is true assume that we wish to operate with a generic, linear K-function with gain g, $K = K_o + gf$, and then choose the anticipation parameter of the ACT policy, A, to be as small as possible, i.e., $A = 1 + g/h$. Under these conditions, the transformed K'-function, given by (5.20a), becomes $K_o + gf - cpf = K_o + gf - Ahf = K_o - hf$. Thus, (5.22b) reduces to $N_{j,n+1} = N_{j,n} - [(N_{j,n} - N_{j-1,n+A}) - K_o] = N_{j-1,n+A} - K_o$. Since $A = 1 + g/h = 1 + G$ we can express the result as:

$$N_{j,n+1} = N_{j-1,n+1+G} + K_o, \qquad (5.23a)$$

which matches (5.15). This is the linear, order-based policy of Example 5.1, which was shown to track the KW target exactly in that example. Since the KW solution is: (i) strongly stable, (ii) monotonic, and (iii) reliable in the sense of (1.5) if the K-function satisfies $inf(K(f)/f) \geq M$, it follows that (5.23a) has these properties too. Therefore, the linear ACT policy with the least possible anticipation is "well behaved," as claimed.

Note as an aside that the first difference of (5.23a) is:

$$Q_{j,n+1} = Q_{j-1,n+1+G}. \qquad (5.23b)$$

This indicates that suppliers simply repeat the orders of their downstream neighbors, but G intervals earlier. With $G = -1$, (5.23b) reduces to the base-stock policy of Example 2.1.

The case where the K-function has zero intercept ($K_o = 0$) and slope equal to the minimum order lag ($g = M$), i.e., where $K = Mf$, deserves special mention because it has the lowest K-curve such that $inf(K(f)/f) \geq M$. As such, it promises low inventories and reliable operation. Indeed, we see from (5.23a) that under this policy the N_j curve is just a horizontally shifted version of the N_{j-1} curve with the smallest feasible shift, $N_{j,n}$= $N_{j-1,n+M/h}$. This is exactly how "lean" supply chains of the "just-in-time" type are operated. In other words, the ACT policy with $K = Mf$ is the JIT method.

Equations (5.23) do not restrict in any way the behavior of the lead supplier "0". Recall that we allow this supplier to operate in any way that will meet demand (e.g., skipping periods to operate more cost effectively), subject to its commitment horizon requirements. The equations only say that the remaining suppliers will act in lockstep ahead of time as per (5.23b). The only requirement for the lead supplier is that it should broadcast its future actions (and stick to them) for a commitment horizon as in (2.16); i.e., of at least $h[JG+1]$ time units. Since under JIT, $M = g \equiv Gh$, we see that the commitment horizon for JIT is $[JM+h]$ time units, as should be expected.

The advantages of operating JIT chains are well known, but they hinge on being able to operate with the required commitment horizon. This may be difficult in cases where M is large. Another disadvantage of JIT systems is that they force the same shipping schedule on all the suppliers, and if the schedule is not appealing to some suppliers they would have to be compensated somehow; e.g., with some pricing mechanism. JIT systems do not fail gracefully, and also suffer the cost of complexity, in particular when suppliers are arranged in networks and produce multiple commodities. JIT robs the suppliers of autonomy. Thus, despite the overwhelming appeal of JIT chains, these notes would not be complete if an analysis of non- JIT systems was not also provided. This is done below.

5.2.4 Properties of the ACT policy: non-linear case

We show here that under certain mild conditions the ACT policy yields monotone, strongly stable and reliable N-curves. The section is structured in a "theorem-proof" format so that it can be skimmed rapidly without loss of continuity.

Theorem 5.1 (Monotonicity and boundedness): If the customer data satisfy $0 \le Q_{0,n} \le Q_{max}$ for all n and the initial asynchronous inventories satisfy $K'(Q_{max}/h) \le K'_{j,0} \le K'(0)$ for all j, then the supplier orders $Q_{j,n}$ and their asynchronous inventories, $K'_{j,n}$, satisfy these inequalities too for all j and all n. This means that orders and inventories are bounded and that the N-curves are monotone. ∎

Proof: As a preliminary step, note that the asynchronous inventories satisfy the recursion: $K'_{j,n+1} = N_{j,n+1} - N_{j-1,n+1+A} = (N_{j,n} + Q_{j,n}) - (N_{j-1,n+A} + Q_{j-1,n+A}) = K'_{j,n} + Q_{j,n} - Q_{j-1,n+A} = K'_{j,n} + hK'^{-1}(K'_{j,n}) - Q_{j-1,n+A}$. If we now define the function $\psi(x) = x + hK'^{-1}(x)$, the recursion is

$$K'_{j,n+1} = \psi(K'_{j,n}) - Q_{j-1,n+A}. \tag{5.24a}$$

Note that ψ is monotone, increasing at a rate between 0 and 1. [This is true because ψ is continuous and piecewise differentiable with derivative: $1 + h/(dK'/dq) = 1 + h/(g-cp) = 1 + 1/(g/h - cp/h) = 1 + 1/(g/h - A) \in [0,1)$. The last relationship of inclusion follows from the stability condition in 5.22), which implies $(g/h - A) \le -1$.] To conclude the preparatory steps, note as well that (5.22a) may be expressed as:

$$Q_{j,n} = hK'^{-1}(K'_{j,n}), \tag{5.24b}$$

where hK'^{-1} is monotone-decreasing. The theorem can now be proven.

This is done for supplier $j = 1$ first. Let $n = 0$ in (5.24a) and note from the conditions of the theorem that the right side of (5.24a) must be in the interval $[\psi(K'(Q_{max}/h)) - Q_{max}, \psi(K'(0))]$, since ψ is monotone and non-decreasing. Furthermore, since $\psi(K'(x)) = K'(x) + xh$, this interval reduces to $[K'(Q_{max}/h), K'(0)]$. Thus, the output of (5.24a) lies in the same interval as its input, and $K'_{1,0}$ satisfies the theorem. If we now iterate (5.24a) for $n = 1, 2, \ldots$, the outputs continue to be in the same interval as the inputs. Thus, all the $K'_{1,n}$ satisfy the theorem.

Consider now (5.24b) for $j = 1$. Since it is a decreasing relation and its inputs satisfy $K'_{1,n} \in [K'(Q_{max}/h), K'(0)]$, it follows that its outputs satisfy $Q_{1,n} \in [hK'^{-1}(K'(0)), hK'^{-1}(K'(Q_{max}/h))] = [0, Q_{max}]$. Thus, the theorem holds for $j = 1$.

We have just shown that supplier $j = 1$ meets the bounds of the theorem if $j = 0$ meets the bounds. The argument of the previous paragraph can now be repeated to show that $j+1$ meets the bounds if j meets them too, and this concludes the proof. ∎

Theorem 5.2 (Strong stability): Under the conditions of Theorem 5.1, the ACT algorithm is strongly stable. ∎

Proof: We have already mentioned that the linearized version of the ACT policy is stable-in-the-small, as per the analysis of Example 4.5. Theorem 5.1 showed that the ACT flows and asynchronous inventories are bounded. Hence, we just have to show that the inventories are bounded. This is true, however, since $K_{jn} = K'_{jn} + (N_{j-1,n+A} - N_{j-1,n}) \le K'(0) + AQ_{max}$. ∎

Conditions guaranteeing the reliability of the ACT algorithm for targets with moderate gains are given below. It will be shown that the algorithm is reliable if the portion of the K-curve corresponding to possible flows, $q \in [0, q_{max}]$, lies above a ray from the origin with slope $\lceil M/h \rceil h$ and also above a ray with slope g_{max}. The following lemma is a preliminary step.

Lemma 5.1: The ACT algorithm with the least possible anticipation (i.e., with $A = cp/h = 1 + g_{max}/h$) is reliable if $g_{max}/h \ge \lceil M/h \rceil$, and $K(q) \ge g_{max}q$. ∎

Proof: It suffices to show that $N_{j,n+1} \ge N_{j-1,n+1+\lceil M/h \rceil}$. To this end, let $\psi(x) = x + hK'^{-1}(x)$, as before, and rewrite (5.22b) as follows:

$$N_{j,n+1} = N_{j-1,n+1+\lceil M/h \rceil} + (N_{j-1,n+A} - N_{j-1,n+1+\lceil M/h \rceil}) + \psi(N_{j,n} - N_{j-1,n+A}).$$

Clearly, it suffices to show that the last two terms on the right side of this equality are non-negative. Since the N-curves are non-decreasing (Theorem 5.1), the second term on the right side will be non-negative if $A \ge 1 + \lceil M/h \rceil$. This is true because $A = 1 + g_{max}/h$ and $g_{max}/h \ge \lceil M/h \rceil$. The third term will be non-negative if $\psi(x) = x + hK'^{-1}(x)$ is non-negative; i.e., if $hK'^{-1}(x) \ge -x$ for all x. Since $K'(x)$ is monotonic decreasing, we apply this transformation to both sides of the inequality after dividing by h and obtain the equivalent condition: $x \le K'(-x/h) \Leftrightarrow -qh \le K'(q) \Leftrightarrow K(q) \ge (cp-h)q = g_{max}q$. Since $K(q) \ge g_{max}q$ by assumption, the third term is also non-negative, and the lemma is proven. ∎

Theorem 5.3 (Reliability): The ACT algorithm with anticipation $A = 1 + \lceil M/h \rceil$ is reliable if the portion of the K-curve corresponding to possible flows, $q \in [0, q_{max}]$, lies above a ray from the origin with slope $\lceil M/h \rceil h$ and also above a ray with slope g_{max}. ∎

Proof: Assume that the portion of the K-curve corresponding to possible flows lies above the two rays, so that $K(q) \ge \lceil M/h \rceil hq$ and $g_{max}q$, and assume too that $g_{max}/h < \lceil M/h \rceil$ so that the lemma cannot be invoked. A K-curve with such a low maximum slope can always be approximated arbitrarily well from above by a new curve with a larger maximum slope; e.g., obtained from a small perturbation in an infinitesimal neighborhood around some q. If we chose the new maximum slope to be $[g_{max}]^{new} = \lceil M/h \rceil h$ the new curve will satisfy the conditions of Lemma 5.1, since $K_{new}(q) \geq K(q) \geq \lceil M/h \rceil hq = [g_{max}]^{new}q$. Thus, if the ACT algorithm is applied with the new K-curve and with anticipation $A^{new} = 1 + [g_{max}]^{new}/h = 1 + \lceil M/h \rceil$, it will be reliable. Since we can chose $K^{new}(q) \to K(q)$, the results with the original curve should be indistinguishable from those obtained with a sufficiently close $K^{new}(q)$, which would be reliable. Hence, we can conclude that the original results are reliable if one chooses $A = 1 + \lceil M/h \rceil$. ∎

It was found in Sec. 5.2.3 that the ACT algorithm is reliable in the linear case if the K-function is reliable. This simple result is consistent with Theorem 5.3, since a linear K- function that satisfies the conditions of the theorem is reliable.

It should be stressed that Theorem 5.3 only states sufficient conditions for reliability and that the ACT policy is also reliable under considerably milder conditions. Of particular interest are situations with gains so large that the g_{max}-ray is above the K-curve for some q's. It turns out that the ACT algorithm is also reliable in this case if (i) the K-function is strictly reliable ($K(q)>Mq$), and (ii) h is sufficiently small. This is true because the ACT algorithm with small h tracks the exact KW solution to within a small time error, η. Therefore, the algorithm will be reliable if the exact solution, u, satisfies (1.5) with M replaced by $M + \eta$. We mentioned in Sec. 5.1 (reliability property of the KW target) that this occurs if the K-function lies above the ray from the origin with slope $M + \eta$. Our claim is based on the fact that η declines towards zero as $h \to 0$. (Thus, if the K-function is strictly above the M-ray it will also be above the $(M+\eta)$-ray for small h).

If h cannot be reduced enough in a particular application to ensure a reasonable reliable operation, then it could be necessary to "raise" the K-function (and operate with larger inventories).

Flex-time applications: Flexible commitment systems have the advantage that their upper bounds can be determined with arbitrarily small h without significant physical consequences. Therefore, it is reasonable to assume that the U-curves are updated so frequent that $\eta \to 0$ if the ACT method is used. Under these conditions, the U-curves satisfy (1.5) if the K-function is strictly reliable. There is no need to adjust the K-function.

Recall, however, that the flex-time method also requires a lower bound, $V_j(t)$, satisfying $U_{j-1}(t+M_j) \leq V_j(t) \leq U_j(t)$. Although (1.5) guarantees that such a lower bound exists, in actual applications we would like to be able to *set* it as low as possible: $V_j(t) = U_{j-1}(t + M_j)$. To do this, however, supplier j would need commitments M_j periods ahead. Thus, the commitment horizon for a reliable operation with tight lower bounds must be at least JM.

We saw earlier that the minimum commitment horizon for stability is Jg_{max}; see (5.22) with $h \to 0$. Therefore, for a flex-time system to be both stable and reliable (with the lowest possible lower bound) its commitment horizon should be at least:

$$\text{Commitment horizon} = [max(M, g_{max})]J. \qquad (5.25)$$

6. Cost Estimation and Optimization

This chapter develops approximate formulae for the operating costs of flex-time (flexible commitment) and discrete-time (rigid commitment) policies, and shows how to choose policies that minimize cost.

We first study in Sec. 6.1 autonomous, flex-time systems where each supplier chooses bounds, $U_j(t)$, (see Sec. 2.4) that approximately minimize their own cost without regard to others; i.e., "user-optimal" bounds.[1] This case is of practical interest because it preserves autonomy and does not ask suppliers to do something that they would not like to do. "User-optimal, flex-time" policies are appealing because they are scalable and can be used with large, complex systems. The chapter does not include a parallel discussion of "user-optimal, discrete-time" policies because in this form of operation suppliers have an incentive to skip intervals by placing large orders – since this reduces the total number of shipments received and the ensuing transportation costs – and this turns out to create problems. The prototypical policy of this type is the order point strategy of Example 2.5, where s and S can be allowed to depend on the N_{j-1}-curve. These policies are problematic for supply chains because they are discontinuous and therefore unstable-in-the-small, as explained at the beginning of Sec. 4.2. Instability makes an analysis of this case mathematically more challenging, albeit possible, but more importantly, it also reduces the appeal of the policies from a practical/system perspective. This is why the "user-optimal, discrete-time" case is not covered in this chapter.

The second part of this chapter (Sec.6.2) examines the case where suppliers act for the benefit of the system, coordinating their operations as necessary. We call this, the "system-optimum" operation. System-optimum results are interesting, even in situations where coordination is not possible, because they give a lower bound to the costs obtained by operating in other ways. Discrete-time systems with rigid commitments are examined first (in Section 6.2.1), and flex-time systems with globally optimized bounds second (in Sec. 6.2.2).

---

[1] The name is adopted following J. Wardrop, the traffic scientist who defined traffic equilibrium as a "game" and noted the congestion "externality" (Wardrop, 1952).

We find that if the input demand changes slowly with time, then the user-optimal and system-optimal costs using flexible commitments are approximately equal.[2] This is quite fortunate. It means that a network of flex-time suppliers can be controlled efficiently in a decentralized way; e.g., with the ACT policy. However, our results also show that that flexibility comes at a cost, since the system-optimum cost under flex-time can be reduced considerably by operating system-optimally with rigid commitments; e.g. by operating in the JIT way.

6.1. Autonomous "user-optimal" operation with flexible commitments

We assume that the upper bound U_j-curves of Fig. 2.3 have been determined with a convergent continuous-time policy (with $h \rightarrow 0$) so that the bounds match perfectly any chosen KW target, $u(x, t)$, for $x = pj$. Recall that in a flex-time operation we defined $K_j = U_j - U_{j-1}$ and $q_j = dU_j/dt$. Thus, K_j and q_j no longer represent the inventories and flows of supplier j. Instead, they are differences and rates of change in the bounds. This notation is logical since we are assuming that actual inventories and order flows cannot be predicted in a flex-time operation, but that the bounds can be predicted since they are a direct result of the policy. The notation is also justified because, as we are about to see, the long run costs can be expressed quite accurately as a function of the bounds alone.

This is most easily seen for inventory costs. It is reasonable to assume that money changes hands across suppliers when the virtual (upper bound) orders are placed.[3] Then, the inventory cost per unit time of supplier j is just a multiple of K_j. As a result, aside from this multiple, the total inventory cost for that supplier is just the integral of K_j over time. If the multiple is the same for all suppliers and we choose the monetary unit so

---

[2] The assumption of slow-varying conditions is made throughout this chapter, but it is only used to derive approximate cost expressions and prove "optimality". The policies that are presented in this chapter can also be used if conditions vary rapidly. Their results should still be reasonably good if this happens. The policies are not exactly optimal for fast-changes because they do not attempt to exploit short-term fluctuations in the input data.

[3] Tying money flow to the bounds is logical because otherwise suppliers would have an incentive to request very high bounds (to give themselves maximum flexibility) and there would not be a counterbalancing penalty. Slight variations on the proposed scheme (still tied to the bounds) could also be reasonable, and they could be analyzed similarly. Our specific choice is based on simplicity.

that the multiple is 1, then the sum of these integrals across j is the total inventory cost. (This sum is also a good approximation for long time periods and large J even if money changes hands in slightly different ways.)

"Rent costs" can also be tied to the bounds. These are the costs associated with the space and facilities needed to hold the items. As explained in Daganzo (1999), these costs are proportional to the maximum (and not the average) item accumulation. If transportation times can be neglected, this is the maximum vertical separation between the S-curves of Fig. 1.1b for adjoining suppliers. If lead times across suppliers are similar, this also equals the maximum vertical separation between pairs of adjoining order curves $\{N_j$ and $N_{j-1}\}$. Note, however, that under flex-time, suppliers would be obliged to reserve enough space to allow for the worst possible timing of the orders, conditional on the bounds. Consideration of Fig. 6.1 shows that the worst case can be accommodated if the storage area of supplier j can hold the maximum vertical separation between U_j and U_{j-2}. (Figure 6.1 assumes that $M=0$ and $V_j(t)=U_{j-1}(t)$, which is a worst-case scenario for rent costs.)   Since the KW target has the property that $sup\{u_j(t)-u_{j-1}(t)\}$ is non-increasing in j, and we are assuming that $U_j \equiv u_j$, we see that $sup\{K_j(t)\}$ will be non-increasing in j. Therefore, $2Jsup\{K_1(t)\}$ is a tight upper bound for the total space needed for all suppliers. This shows that rent costs, like inventory costs, can also be estimated independently of the N_j curves. This is also true if the chain is inhomogeneous. To keep the discussion focused, however, rent costs will be neglected from now on.[4]

It turns out that the production and transportation costs (including re-order costs) for supplier j can too be expressed in terms of U_j and U_{j-1}. Since the bounds fix the inventory costs, independently of when the actual orders are made, suppliers will try to time the latter so as to minimize their production and transportation costs (conditional on the bounds). For example, if suppliers experience a fixed cost per order and another fixed cost per item produced, their response would be obvious. Since the total production cost is independent of their actions (the total number of items produced is given), they would simply try to minimize the number of orders by waiting until the last minute to place an order and then ordering the maximum amount possible. The strategy is shown on Fig. 6.1, which displays the case where $M = 0$. For cases with $M_j > 0$, the supplier would choose its most favorable lower bound, $V_j(t) = U_{j-1}(t+ M_j)$, and the N_j-curve would then bounce between $U_j(t)$ and $U_{j-1}(t+ M_j)$. Clearly, for any given

---

[4]   This is reasonable if items are expensive. In other cases, the results can be easily general-ized by including terms of the form: $2Jsup\{K_1(t)\}$ in the objective function.

M_j, curves U_j and U_{j-1} determine the long run costs of production and transportation. This should also be true in cases where suppliers have other cost structures.

Let us now derive an expression for the user-optimum cost per unit time of a chain operating in steady state. It follows from the above discussion that if we are given two steady-state curves U_j and U_{j-1}, the total (inventory, production and transportation) cost per unit time of supplier j is just a function of these curves, and the value of M_j. Since the two curves are parallel straight lines, this cost can be expressed as a function of only two variables, the separation between curves, $U_j - U_{j-1} = K_j$ and their slope, $dU_j/dt = q$. We denote this function $Z_j(K, q)$ (*cost per unit time*).

Recall, though, that supplier j sees U_{j-1} as data, but it can choose U_j. Thus, in a "user-optimum" solution the supplier would try to choose its best K for the given q. It is assumed that suppliers are only allowed to choose monotone U-functions guaranteeing (1.5); i.e., such that $U_j(t) \geq U_{j-1}(t+M_j)$. We know that this occurs if K (the vertical separation between

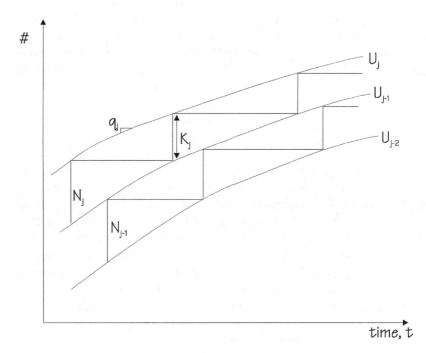

Figure 6.1. Storage considerations for a flex-time supply chain with a negligible minimum order lag: $M=0$

U-curves) and q satisfy $K \geq Mq$. Let $K_{(j)}(q)$ be the value of K that minimizes $Z_j(K, q)$ for a given q, subject to $K_{(j)}(q) \geq M_j q$, and call $K_{(j)}(q)$ the "user-optimum K-function". Define too the "user-optimum cost function" $Z^*_j(q) = Z_j(K_{(j)}(q), q)$. The sum of this expression across j is an estimate for the steady-state cost per unit time for the complete chain. These steady-state expressions can now be used to approximate the costs for the dynamic case.

To do this we use the KW model, since the U_j-curves match the KW targets exactly. We first associate a continuous space variable x with the discrete supplier variable j and then eliminate j from the notation. Therefore, we replace the user-optimum K-functions $K_{(j)}(q)$ by a smooth function of space, $\rho = \rho(f, x)$, with units of "items/distance". This function is defined by $\rho(q, jp) = K_{(j)}(q)/p \geq M(x)q/p$. We also replace $Z_j(K, q)$ by a smooth cost density function $z(\rho, f, x)$ with units of "monetary units/time-distance", such that $z(K/p, q, jp) = Z_j(K, q)/p$. This last equality ensures that the integral of the cost density over x and t approximately equals the sum of the total supplier costs over suppliers and time. Therefore, the total cost is:

$$\text{Cost} \cong \int_{x,t} z(\rho, f, x)\, dxdt = \int_{x,t} z(\rho(f, x), f, x)\, dxdt. \tag{6.1}$$

The second equality is justified because in the KW solution, density must be consistent with flow everywhere, $\rho = \rho(f, x)$, except on shocks.[5] The unknown f should now be eliminated from (6.1). This is easy in the linear case, because then $f(x, t)$ is the same at all locations except for a time displacement equal to the wave trip time between 0 and x, $\tilde{g}(x)$; i.e., $f(x, t) = q_0(t + \tilde{g}(x))$.[6] By changing the time variable in (6.1), using $t' = t + \tilde{g}(x)$, we see that f becomes $q_0(t')$ in (6.1) and the integral simplifies to:

---

[5] This fact was expressed by means of (5.3) in Sec. 5.1, which pertained to homogeneous problems. The fact is also true for inhomogeneous problems.

[6] To see that this is true, first differentiate the inhomogeneous version of (5.5b), with g_j substituted for g, which yields $f_j(t) = f_{j-1}(t+g_j) = q_0(t+ \tilde{g}_j)$, where $\tilde{g}_j = g_1 + g_2 + \ldots + g_j$. Then, express the result in continuous space, which becomes $f(x, t) = q_0(t+\tilde{g}(x))$, where $\tilde{g}(x)$ is a smooth function such that $\tilde{g}(jp) = \tilde{g}_j$.

$$\text{Cost} \cong \int_{x,t'} z\big(\rho(q_0,x),q_0,x\big)dxdt' \cong \sum_{j}\int_{t'} Z_j\big(K_{(j)}(q_0),q_0\big)dt' =$$

$$= \sum_{j}\int_{t'} Z_j^*(q_0)\,dt' \tag{6.2a}$$

The second equality of (6.2a) is obtained by returning to discrete space (using jp instead of x), and the third one by the definition of $Z^*_j(q)$.

For a homogeneous system the result is:

$$\text{Cost} \cong \int_{t} z\big(\rho(q_0),q_0\big)Jpdt \cong J\int_{t} Z\big(K(q_0),q_0\big)dt$$

$$\cong J\int_{t} Z^*(q_0)\,dt \quad \text{(if homogeneous).} \tag{6.2b}$$

Errors in these approximations arise when the system strays far from a steady state due to rapid changes in the demand rate. The errors can be shown to be negligible if the customer N-curve can be approximated well by a smooth curve $u_0(t)$ with low curvature; i.e. such that its slope changes very little in a wave trip time across suppliers: $[dq_0/dt]g^2 \ll 1$. The expressions are also good approximations for non-linear systems.

A note about uncertainty: The discussion up to this point assumed perfect information. This does not mean that there can be no uncertainty; only that the lead supplier (or the customer) must always be committed to an upper bound for future orders in the commitment horizon of the chain. Such commitments may require safety stocks, and the associated costs would have to be included in (6.2). In most cases, the safety stock cost should be proportional to the square root of the commitment horizon, which, according to (4.15); is of order Jg. Thus,

$$\text{Safety stock cost} \cong \int_{t} O((Jg)^{\frac{1}{2}})dt. \tag{6.2c}$$

Note from (6.2b) and (6.2c) that the deterministic costs of a user-optimum supply chain are of order J, but the costs due to uncertainty are of order $J^{1/2}$.

All the results derived so far pertain to supply chains where suppliers act in their own self-interest by operating with a stable policy that allows them operate with minimal cost. This, however, does not imply that the overall system's costs are minimized. The remainder of this chapter addresses this issue.

6.2. Coordinated "system-optimum" operation: Optimization

Here we consider systems for which coordination is possible. We will examine first rigid systems operated without any flexibility, such as JIT systems, and then systems that allow for some flexibility in the placement of orders. To be as general as possible, and be able to claim that the results are truly optimal, we will assume (even in the rigid case) that every supplier can place an order at any time, i.e. that the system is operated in continuous time ($h \to 0$). Flexibility is introduced by means of bounds, such as those of Fig. 2.3, which are globally optimized, also in continuous time. Our goal is finding the set of N-curves (in the rigid case) or U-curves (in the flexible case) that minimize total cost, subject to reliability and monotonicity constraints. Stability is not an issue any more, since unstable solutions cannot be optimal.

6.2.1 Rigid operation: JIT systems

6.2.1.1 Homogeneous chains

In the rigid operation case, the N-curves of an optimally run homogeneous chain should be translationally symmetric; i.e., they should satisfy (5.23). Under translational symmetry, the long-run production and transportation costs of all suppliers should be identical to that of the lead supplier, independent of the parameters used in (5.23). Therefore, these parameters (K_o and G) should be chosen so as to minimize the inventory costs, subject to the reliability constraint (1.5). It should be clear that this is achieved by the JIT values ($K_o = 0$ and $Gh = M$), since under JIT each item spends the least possible amount of time (M) between suppliers. Therefore, for the rest of this subsection we restrict our attention to the JIT case.

The only decision variables of a JIT system are the order sizes and reorder intervals of the lead supplier (in continuous time) since these variables determine the N_1-curve, and this curve determines the others. (The lead supplier is numbered "1" from now on.) It should be stressed that the reorder instants are not required to be on a lattice and the reorder intervals can be irregular. There is total flexibility in choosing N_1.

Under JIT, every item spends a fixed time, $(J-1)M$, making its way to the lead supplier, and then another time at the this supplier waiting to be consumed. The latter time includes two components: (i) the time an item needs to work its way through the safety stock of the lead supplier, which is needed to ensure that the supplier does not lose too many customers by keeping its commitments, and (ii) a "waiting" or "load-make-up" time that depends on the time between orders.[7] In most cases, component (i) should be proportional to the square root of the commitment horizon, and component (ii) should average ½ of the typical reorder interval. To a first order of approximation, the decision variables of a JIT system (the reorder intervals) do not affect component (i); see for example the discussion in Daganzo (1999), Sec. 2.5. Thus, in a steady state with reorder interval H, the average of the total time in process across all items is of the form: $H/2 + (J-1)M + O((JM)^{½})$.

The reorder cost is also easy to calculate since a JIT system has J reorders (one per supplier) in each reorder interval. If there is a fixed reorder cost, π, with each order, the reorder cost per interval is $J\pi$. For a steady state system with demand rate, q, exactly qH, items are consumed in an interval. Therefore, the average reorder cost per item is: $J\pi/qH$. If in addition there is a fixed production/handling cost per item (combined for all suppliers), π_0, then this constant should be added to the total, although it should not influence the choice of H.

If we use monetary units such that the inventory cost per item equals the time spent, then the sum of the average inventory, handling and reorder costs per item is: $H/2 + J\pi/qH + \pi_0 + (J-1)M + O((JM)^{½})$. This is minimized for $H^* = (2J\pi/q)^{½}$, and the optimum average cost per item is then: $(2J\pi/q)^{½} + \pi_0 + (J-1)M + O((JM)^{½})$. The cost per unit time is $q[(2J\pi/q)^{½} + \pi_0 + (J-1)M + O((JM)^{½})]$.

When the system is not in a steady state but the demand varies slowly, an approximation for the optimum cost of operating the system for a long time is obtained by integrating the above expression for the cost per unit time, as if the system had been in a steady state. The result for the interval $(-\infty, T_o)$ is:

---

[7] The waiting time arises when customer demand is continuous over time (or nearly continuous) but the deliveries to the lead supplier occur in batches at discrete times. Even in the most favorable case, where items in a batch were delivered to the lead supplier as its inventory ran out, the items would still have to wait for the arrival of their customer. If customers arrive uniformly over time, the waiting time is about ½ of the interval between deliveries.

$$\text{Cost*} \cong \int_{t=-\infty}^{T_o} \{[2J\pi q_0(t)]^{1/2} + \pi_0 q_0(t) + (J\text{-}1)Mq_0(t) +$$

$$+ O((JM)^{1/2})q_0(t)\}\,dt. \qquad (6.3)$$

The first term of this expression is the sum of the "waiting" and the "re-order" costs. Note that this term increases with the unit cost per reorder and the length of the chain as $[2J\pi]^{1/2}$. This is the main advantage of rigidly synchronized chains, for we will see in Sec. 6.2.2.2 that the cost expression for system-optimum, flexible systems is almost identical to (6.3), except for the first term, which increases proportionately with the length of the chain, as $2J[\pi]^{1/2}$.

The same effect arises in the autonomous case, as can be seen most easily by writing (6.2b) for the case with $M = 0$, using the current set of assumptions and ignoring uncertainty. The user-optimum K is determined with an "economic order quantity" trade-off, which yields $K(q) = (q\pi)^{1/2}$. Therefore, the supplier cost is $Z^*(q) = 2(q\pi)^{1/2} + q\pi_0/J$ and we find:

$$\text{Cost*} \cong \int_{t=-\infty}^{T_o} \{2J[\pi q_0(t)]^{1/2} + \pi_0 q_0(t)\}\,dt \qquad (6.2d)$$

for the autonomous case with $M = 0$ and no uncertainty.

6.2.1.2 Inhomogeneous chains:

The JIT system can also be used with inhomogeneous chains, with similar results. In fact, reconsideration of our previous arguments shows that expression (6.3) continues to hold, if the constants π and M appearing on its right side are replaced by their averages across suppliers.

In the inhomogeneous case, however, translational symmetry is not necessarily optimum; cost may be reduced further if suppliers with high reorder costs are allowed to ship less frequently, but still "in synch" with the others. Because an optimization allowing for these degrees of freedom is somewhat involved, and not strictly needed for the qualitative comparisons that are the goal of this chapter, it is not included here.

6.2.2. Flexible operation with "system-optimum" bounds

Here we look for an optimum set of bounds, $U_j(t) \geq U_{j-1}(t+M_j)$, assuming that each supplier j is allowed to choose any N_j that remains between $U_j(t)$ and $V_j(t) = U_{j-1}(t+M_j)$, as shown in Fig. 2.3. As in Sec. 6.1, we will assume perfect information and will discuss the effect of uncertainty at the end. Recall that the bounds must satisfy $U_j(t) \geq U_{j-1}(t+M_j)$ to ensure that the N-curves satisfy feasibility condition (1.5). For simplicity of notation, it will be assumed below that $M_j = 0$, i.e., that $U_j(t) \geq U_{j-1}(t)$, but it should be noted that a solution with $M_j > 0$ can always be obtained from the one about to be presented by shifting the bound curves; i.e., using for the jth curve, $U_j(t+M_j+M_{j-1}+M_{j-2}+...)$. Consideration shows that the cost added by this transformation is given by the third term of (6.3). Since the contributions to cost from strictly positive M_j's are equal in the JIT and flex-time cases, an analysis with $M_j = 0$ illustrates most transparently the differences between the two approaches.

We continue to assume that money changes hands across suppliers when the U-orders are placed (perhaps with a delay), and that suppliers minimize their reorder costs by ordering as infrequently as possible; i.e., using N-curves that bounce between the upper and lower bounds as in Fig. 6.1. As before, both the inventory and optimum reorder costs can be expressed as a function of the U-curves, and one can just look for the optimum set of curves.

The resulting optimization problem is difficult. It can be cast as a calculus of variations problem for J unknown functions, $U(t) = (U_1(t)$, $U_2(t)$, ..., $U_J(t))$, but the objective function is non-convex and the solution not unique. Thus, we will attempt to find *all* the solutions satisfying the first order conditions of the calculus of variations problem and then pick the best with a different method. We have found a way of doing this by treating the supplier number as a continuous variable (as in Sec. 6.1) and then using a two-dimensional calculus of variations device for the optimization. The result is a neat closed form formula for the complete solution. Because this approach can also be tried with other multidimensional problems with a dynamic programming structure, the description in this section will be a bit more detailed than needed in the interest of clarity. It is divided in three parts: formulation; solution of the homogeneous problem; and solution of the inhomogeneous problem.

6.2.2.1. Formulation

Instead of a set of J curves, $U(t)$, we now look for a single function of two variables, $u(x, t)$, with the understanding that the $U_j(t)$ are given by the values of u on the lattice: $U_j(t) = u(jp, t)$. The expression to be minimized is the same as before:

$$\text{Cost} = \int_{x,t} z(\rho, f, x)\, dx\, dt .$$ (6.4a)

where, $z(\rho, f, x)$ continues to be a cost density function with units of "monetary units/time-distance," and ρ and f are the partial derivatives of u. This is the same objective as (6.1), but here ρ and f are not linked by the KW relation. This is why a lower cost can be obtained. The following constrains must be satisfied:

$$u(0, t) = N_0(t), \qquad \text{(boundary condition)} \qquad (6.4b)$$

and

$$f = \partial u / \partial t \geq 0 , \ \rho = \partial u / \partial x \geq 0 \quad \text{(monotonicity and reliability.)} \qquad (6.4c)$$

The second inequality of (6.4c) is needed to ensure that (1.5) is satisfied with $M = 0$. It is assumed that $dN_0(t)/dt = q_0(t) \geq 0$, and that this function is "slow-varying." [8]

We assume that the cost density, z, is the sum of: (*i*) an inventory cost proportional to ρ, (*ii*) a production/handling cost proportional to f, and (*iii*) a reorder cost proportional to f/ρ. These relationships should be evident from Fig. 6.1. For example, the figure clearly shows that the reorder interval of supplier j at time t is approximately $K_j(t)/f_j(t)$. Hence the reorder rate is $f_j(t)/K_j(t)$, and the reorder rate per unit space, $f_j(t)/K_j(t)p \cong f/\rho p^2$. This is in agreement with (*iii*). If monetary units are chosen so that the inventory constant is unity, and we allow costs (*ii*) and (*iii*) to depend on the supplier, i.e., on x, the general expression for z is:[9]

$$z = \rho + f\, s(x)[r_0(x) + r_1/\rho], \qquad (6.5)$$

where $s(x)$, $r_0(x)$, $r_1 > 0$. We have chosen to factor out coefficient $s(x)$ and to retain r_1 as a constant, because this simplifies slightly some of the

---

[8] This is not a strong assumption because in real applications the input data will usually be the upper bound of the lead supplier, $U_1(t)$, rather than the customer demand. Since this bound is ultimately a decision variable, we are in essence restricting ourselves to the space of solutions where the second derivative of the input bound is small.

[9] This assumes that the inventory carrying cost per supplier is the same across suppliers (i.e., that suppliers do not ad value to the items they process). Otherwise, the first term would have to depend on x too.

expressions about to be derived. In the homogeneous case we will use $s(x) = 1$ and $r_0(x) = r_0$. Note from its dimensions that r_1 is related to the fixed reorder cost π, of Sec. 6.2.1.1 by $r_1 p^2 = \pi$. Likewise r_0, in the homogenous case, is related to π_0 by $\pi_0 = r_0 Jp$.

Equations (6.4) and (6.5) define a two-dimensional problem in the calculus of variations. The stationary solutions of such problems satisfy the 2-dimensional version of Euler's equation, which in our case is:

$$\partial z_p / \partial x + \partial z_f / \partial t = 0. \tag{6.6}$$

[This equation is obtained by taking the first variation of (6.4) and then using Green's formula; see, e.g., Courant and Hilbert (1953).]

As customary, we shall use x and t subscripts to denote partial derivatives. Combining (6.5) and (6.6) we find:

$$-sr_1 f_x / \rho^2 - s' r_1 f / \rho^2 + 2sr_1 f \rho_x / \rho^3 - sr_1 \rho_t / \rho^2 = 0 ,$$

where s' is the derivative of $s(x)$. Note from (6.4c) that $f_x = \rho_t$. Hence, if we substitute f_x for ρ_t in the above, and then divide both sides by $-sr_1 f/\rho^2$ we find the equivalent expression, $2(f_x / f) + [s'/s - 2\rho_x / \rho] = 0$. The left side of this equality can be integrated with respect to x so that the equation becomes

$$\partial / \partial x \, [\, 2ln f + ln s - 2ln \rho] = 0. \tag{6.7}$$

Since the quantity in brackets can only be a function of t, the solution must satisfy:

$$s^{1/2} f/\rho = \phi(t) \iff u_t / u_x = \phi(t) / s^{1/2} \iff u_t - [\phi(t) / s^{1/2}] u_x = 0 \tag{6.8}$$

for any non-negative $\phi(t)$. (Non-negativity is required because $s^{1/2}$, f and ρ are non-negative.)

The last equality of (6.8) is a first order, linear, partial differential equation in u that has a unique solution when subject to boundary condition (6.4b) (Cauchy data). We see that the left member of the last equality of (6.8) is the total derivative of u with respect to t along any curve with slope,

$$dx/dt = [-\phi(t) / s^{1/2}]. \tag{6.9}$$

Curves that satisfy these conditions are called "characteristics." (This is the same concept as the "waves" we encountered with the KW model.) Because our equation is homogeneous, u is constant along the characteristics. This means that a characteristic is simply the space-time trajectory of the acknowledgement for a specific bound number. The complete family of trajectories/characteristics fills the space. It can be obtained by integrating (6.9) after separating variables. To express the result in a short form, we define:[10]

$$\Phi(t) = \int_0^t \phi(w)\,dw \quad \text{and} \quad S(x) = \int_0^x s^{\frac{1}{2}}(w)\,dw. \tag{6.10}$$

Then, the curve passing through boundary point $(0, t_0)$ can be expressed as:

$$\Phi(t) + S(x) = \Phi(t_0), \tag{6.11}$$

since this expression satisfies (6.9). Note that $S(x)$ is data.

Since the (constant) value of u along a characteristic is the value of N_0 at its source, and since the time at the source for the characteristic passing through an arbitrary point (x, t) is $t_0 = \Phi^{-1}(\Phi(t) + S(x))$, we see that the value of u at an arbitrary point must be:

$$u(x, t) = N_0(\Phi^{-1}(\Phi(t) + S(x))). \tag{6.12}$$

This is the solution we sought.

Equation (6.12) characterizes *all* the stationary solutions of our calculus of variations problem, including all local optima. We should now determine which Φ is globally optimum among the class of differentiable, non-decreasing functions. The homogeneous problem is solved first. It is then shown that every inhomogeneous problem can be reduced to an equivalent homogeneous problem, and a general formula based on this principle is given.

6.2.2.2. The homogeneous problem.

For homogeneous problems $r_0(x)$ is constant, $s(x) = 1$ and $S(x) = x$. Thus, the characteristics are:

---

[10] The capital letter "S" was used earlier in connection with the S-curves. It is used here again because the S-curves are not used in this section.

$$\Phi(t) + x = \Phi(t_0),\tag{6.13}$$

and the cost density function is:

$$z = \rho + f[r_0 + r_1/\rho].\tag{6.14}$$

Our goal is finding the Φ that minimizes

$$\text{Cost} = \int_{x,t}\left(\rho + f[r_0 + r_1/\rho]\right)dxdt,\tag{6.15}$$

where $\rho \equiv u_x$ and $f \equiv u_t$ are related to Φ through the derivatives of (6.12).

To solve the problem, we first eliminate f from (6.15) using the identity $f = \rho\phi(t)$. (This identity holds because, with $S(x) = x$, the partial derivatives of (6.12) satisfy $u_t / u_x = \phi(t)$.) Hence,

$$\text{Cost} = \int_{x,t}\left(\rho + r_0\rho\phi(t) + r_1\phi(t)\right)dxdt.\tag{6.16}$$

We now find from (6.12) that the expression for ρ is

$$\rho = u_x = N_0{}'(\Phi^{-1}(\Phi(t) + x))[\Phi^{-1}{}'(\Phi(t) + x)],\tag{6.17}$$

where we have used primes to denote derivatives. To simplify the notation, let us now use $t_0(x, t)$ for the time when the characteristic passing through (x, t) intersects the time axis, as per (6.13); i.e.:

$$t_0 = \Phi^{-1}(\Phi(t) + x).\tag{6.18}$$

Therefore, (6.17) can be rewritten as:

$$\rho = N_0{}'(t_0)[\Phi^{-1}{}'(\Phi(t_0))] = q_0(t_0)/\phi(t_0).\tag{6.19}$$

If $q_0(t)$ varies slowly, it is reasonable to look for solutions where $\phi(t)$ also varies slowly. We can then approximate $q_0(t_0)$ by $q_0(t)$ and $\phi(t_0)$ by $\phi(t)$ in the above, so that we can use $q_0(t)/\phi(t)$ for ρ in (6.16), instead of $q_0(t_0)/\phi(t_0)$. Note that the new integrand of (6.16) is independent of x. Thus, we can integrate (6.16) with respect to x, and find:

$$\text{Cost} \cong \int_{t=-\infty}^{T_o} [q_0(t)/\phi(t) + r_0q_0(t) + r_1\phi(t)]Jpdt .$$
(6.20)

This expression is minimized by the value of $\phi(t)$, $\phi^*(t)$, that minimizes its integrand for every t. Hence, we choose:

$$\phi^*(t) = [q_0(t)/r_1]^{\frac{1}{2}} \quad \text{and} \quad \Phi^*(t) \cong \int_{w=0}^{t} [q_0(w)/r_1]^{\frac{1}{2}}dt.$$
(6.21)

Note that, as desired, $\phi^*(t)$ varies slowly.

Equation (6.21) gives the answer we were seeking, Φ^*. The equation also allows us to express the (near) optimal solution as:

$$u^*(x, t) = N_0(\Phi^{*-1}(\Phi^*(t) + x))), \quad \text{and}$$
(6.22)

$$\text{Cost*} \cong \int_{t=-\infty}^{T_o} (2[r_1q_0(t)]^{\frac{1}{2}} + r_0q_0(t))Jpdt \quad \text{(if } q_0 \text{ varies slowly).}$$
(6.23)

Note now that if the chain had been autonomous with $M = 0$, and each supplier had determined its U-curves user-optimally with the K-function that minimizes their steady state cost, then the resulting cost would have been given by (6.2d) at the end of sec 6.2.1. Recalling that the parameters π and π_0 in (6.2d) are related to r_1 and r_0 by $\pi = r_1p^2$ and $\pi_0 = r_0Jp$, we immediately see that (6.2d) and (6.23) coincide. This establishes that if the input varies slowly and suppliers maximize their own benefit by using a user-optimum ACT rule (or any other rule that approximates the user-optimum KW target) then the resulting cost is approximately system-optimal.

A comparison of (6.23) with the first two terms of JIT expression (6.3) (continuing to assume that $M = 0$) confirms the statement made at the end of sec. 6.2.1: that a JIT system should have a smaller cost than a flex-time system. The comparative advantage of a JIT system grows with J.

A note about commitment horizons: One can see from (6.22) that the actions of the upstream supplier, $(x = Jp)$ at time t are determined by customer data at a future time, $t_0 = \Phi^{-1}(\Phi(t) + Jp) \geq t$. Therefore, if the demand is uncertain, the future needs to be anticipated. This can be done in a number of ways; for example, by forcing the first supplier to commit to future bounds for a rolling interval (t, t_0). The length of this rolling interval is:

Commitment horizon $= \Phi^{-1}(\Phi(t) + Jp) - t.$ (6.24)

If the first supplier commits in this way, the rest of the chain can then be run with bounds that are system-optimum, conditional on the complete U-curve of the lead supplier. Of course, the optimization is not complete until a *slow-varying* lead U-curve is determined. The best U-curve would minimize the sum of three terms: the supply chain costs (6.23), the safety stock cost of the lead supplier, which should be of order $O((t_0-t)^{\frac{1}{2}})$ given the required rolling horizon, and the opportunity cost of missed sales due to insufficient inventories. Since the last two components of this sum are given by conventional (single-supplier) methods of inventory theory, we see that the supply chain problem has been reduced to a standard single supplier problem.

This simplification also holds for autonomous systems operated with user-optimum bounds, and for JIT systems. The only modifications are: (i) that the commitment horizons are now different, and (ii) that either (6.2) or the first three terms of (6.3) should be used instead of (6.23) to evaluate the deterministic cost of the supply chain. The commitment horizon for the JIT scheme is $MJ = 0$ (since we are assuming that $M = 0$). The commitment horizon with autonomous, user-optimum bounds (the ACT policy with $h \to 0$) is $g_{max}J$; see (5.22). With slow-varying inputs, the commitment horizon for system optimum operation turns out to be about $2gJ$, i.e., about twice as large as for the user-optimum case.[11] Finally, note that flexible operations require longer horizons than JIT, and therefore larger safety stocks.

A comment about lead times: We have assumed in all of the above that $M = 0$, but the qualitative conclusions of Sec. 6.2.2 are general. As mentioned at the outset of that section, a solution with $M_j > 0$ would include extra inventory costs that could be estimated by shifting in time the U-curves for $M = 0$. Since these shifts are the same for all strategies, the added costs due to non-zero M's are similar across strategies.[12]

---

[11] The reader should remember that $g = \frac{1}{2}p[r_1/q]^{\frac{1}{2}}$ when manipulating (6.24) to reproduce this result.

[12] The added costs are not exactly the same because the portion of total cost due to uncertainty is non-linear in M; in all cases, this portion is given by the last term of (6.3) with $O((JM)^{\frac{1}{2}})$ replaced by $O((JM+ horizon)^{\frac{1}{2}})$.

6.2.2.3. The inhomogeneous problem.

The only difference here is that in the minimization problem (6.4) the cost, z, now includes the space dependent functions $s(x)$ and $r_0(x)$, as in (6.5); i.e.,

$$z = u_x + u_t\, s\, [r_0 + r_1/u_x]. \tag{6.25}$$

Fortunately, the current minimization problem can be reduced to an equivalent homogeneous problem through the change of variable:

$$x' = S(x) \qquad \Leftrightarrow \qquad x = S^{-1}(x'), \tag{6.26}$$

where $S(x)$ is given by (6.10), and the mapping that converts every function $u(x, t)$ into a function $u'(x', t) = u(x, t)$ with the same cost. We shall look for u'^* and then undo the conversion.

The total cost is:

$$\text{Cost} = \int_{x,t}\left(u_x + u_t s(x)[r_0(x) + r_1/u_x]\right)dx dt \tag{6.27}$$

$$= \int_{x',t}\left(u'_{x'} + u'_t[r_0(S^{-1}(x'))s(S^{-1}(x'))^{1/2} + r_1/u'_{x'}]\right)dx'dt \tag{6.28}$$

which should be minimized subject to

$$u'(0, t) = N_0(t). \tag{6.29}$$

Note that (6.28) has the structure of the cost equation for a homogeneous problem, except for the first term of the quantity in brackets, which still depends on x. This is quite satisfactory because this term does not appear in the Euler equation; see (6.6) and the ensuing derivation. Hence, the characteristics of the transformed problem Ψ are those of a homogeneous problem, and still satisfy (6.13):

$$\Psi(t) + x' = \Psi(t_0). \tag{6.30}$$

The derivations following (6.13) can now be repeated, and we find:

$$\Psi^*(t) \cong \int_{w=-\infty}^{t} [q_0(w)/r_1]^{1/2}dt. \tag{6.31}$$

This yields the desired solution for the transformed problem:

$$u'(x', t) = N_0(\Psi^{*-1}(\Psi^*(t) + x')).$$

Therefore, the solution in the original coordinate system is:

$$u(x, t) = N_0(\Psi^{*-1}(\Psi^*(t) + S(x))). \tag{6.32}$$

Using the same logic as in the inhomogenous case, we now derive a cost expression. First, we find that, for slow-varying inputs, the derivatives of u are: $u_t \cong q_0(t)$ and $u_x \cong [q_0(t)/\psi(t)]s(x)^{1/2}$, where $\psi(t) = d\Psi(t)/dt$. When these expressions are inserted in (6.27) and the result is minimized with respect to $\psi(t)$ we obtain the desired cost expression:

$$\text{Cost*} \cong S(Jp) \int_{t=-\infty}^{T_o} 2[r_1 q_0(t)]^{1/2} \, dt + [\int_{t=-\infty}^{T_o} q_0(t)dt][\int_{x=0}^{Jp} r_0(x)s(x)dx]. \tag{6.33}$$

Note that this formula reduces to (6.23) if, as occurs in the homogeneous case, $s(x) = 1$, $S(x) = x$ and $r_0(x) = r_0$. Equations (6.32) and (6.33) give the general system-optimum solution for the inhomogeneous supply chain problem with flexible shipments.

A comment about "value-added" chains: Recall from (6.5) and (6.25) that the inhomogeneous effects were not allowed to occur in the first term of the cost function, which captures inventory costs. Since inventory costs are assumed to be the same for all suppliers, our results do not apply to systems where the items change character (and value) as they flow along the supply chain. To handle these types of problems one would have to introduce a location specific coefficient, $\sigma(x)$, for the first term of (6.25). This more general problem can also be reduced to a simple problem through a change of variable. Instead of (6.26), one should now choose the change of x-variable that will make the coefficients of the first and third terms of the integrand in (6.28) equal. The resulting problem is still inhomogeneous but simpler—since the inhomogeneity now takes the form of a different cost weight for each supplier rather than a change in item character. Under these conditions, the user-optimum solution with a slow-varying input should still be approximately system-optimal.[13]   This solution would automatically "hoard" inventories at the locations and

---

[13] The user-optimum cost expressions are not given here to avoid repetitiveness. They can be easily derived since the user-optimum rule for the transformed problem is independent of the weights.

times where it would be cheapest, but would not be user-optimal for the untransformed problem; i.e., inventories would sometimes have to be kept with unwilling suppliers. Therefore, suitable contracts would have to be negotiated, as occurs in the JIT case.

7. Discussion

7.1 Extensions: Multi-commodity networks

The results in this document can be easily extended to production networks of one and multiple commodities. A full development of these ideas is possible, but only the logic and the main results are given below.

For systems that produce a single commodity for a single final supplier; e.g., when producing generic "cars" at a single assembly line, a supply network will usually be a directed tree (graph) with a supplier at each node and the final customer (e.g., the assembly line) at its root. The graph may include "ordinary" suppliers that receive items from single nodes, and also "merge" suppliers that receive items from more than one node; see Fig. 7.1a and 7.1b. Suppliers of both types should send items to only one node. For systems of this type, it can be assumed without loss of generality that merge nodes require exactly one input item from each input arc to produce one output item. [No generality is lost since the definition of "item" is up to us, and one can always define "item" as that quantity of supplies that is required to make a unit of final product. For example, if a car requires 5 wheels to be produced, one can simply define an item as a set of 5 wheels.]

When dealing with networks, it is convenient to index the flows by arc label (i, j); e.g., so that the cumulative number of order acknowledgements sent on (i, j) by time t becomes $N_{ij}(t)$. Then, the autonomous, anticipative policy with canonical form (2.15) would be expressed as:

$$Q_{ij,n} = H_{ij}(K_{ij,n}, Q_{jk,n+A-1}, Q_{jk,n+A-2}, \ldots) - K_{ij,n} \quad \text{for all } j. \tag{7.1a}$$

$$K_{ij,n+1} = H_{ij}(K_{ij,n}, Q_{jk,n+A-1}, Q_{jk,n+A-2}, \ldots) - Q_{jk,n} \quad \text{for all } j \tag{7.1b}$$

where "k" is the downstream node from j. Also as before, H_{ij} should be such that condition (1.5) is satisfied. Note that (7.1) determines the N-curves on a single path of the tree independent of anything on other paths. Thus, if a choice of $\{H_{ij}\}$ for all the arcs of the network yields a stable solution for all the paths of the tree, the complete system will be stable. This will happen for example if we use the ACT rule (5.22c):

$$Q_{ij,n} = hK_{ij}'^{-1}(N_{ij,n} - N_{jk,n+Aj})$$

$$\text{(with } K_{ij}'(f) = K_{ij}(f) - A_{ij}hf, \text{ and integer } A_{ij} \geq 1 + g_{ij,max}/h). \tag{7.2}$$

The path-independence logic also reveals that if a set of policies $\{H_{ij}\}$ is reliable, monotone and bounded for the paths of the network, then these properties must also hold for the network as a whole. The ACT rule (7.2), in particular, exhibits these properties.

System costs can also be easily estimated. If $Z_j(K, q)$ is the steady-state cost per unit time of supplier j when its inventory level is K and the demand rate is q, and $Z^*_j(q)$ the resulting cost if the inventory is optimally chosen, then the cost of an autonomous, user-optimum operation with flexible shipments is still given by (6.2a):

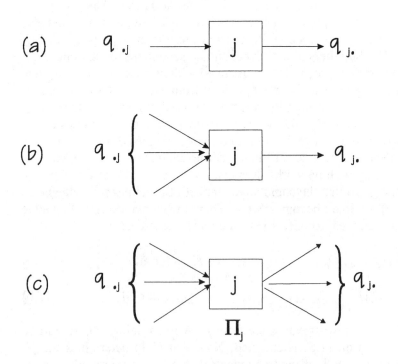

Figure 7.1. Different supplier types: (a) ordinary; (b) "merge"; (c) "combination"

$$\text{Cost} \cong \sum_j \int_t Z_j^*\big(q_0(t)\big)dt . \tag{7.3}$$

The cost results for centralized operations can be similarly extended. In the JIT case for example, the only change to (6.3) is that costs should be summed over the whole tree, and the commitment horizon would depend on the path with the longest processing time.

Multi-product networks can be treated similarly, using a superposition of trees. Here, however, we need to introduce "combination" suppliers that can receive inputs from different nodes and produce different outputs, also for different nodes; see Fig. 7.1c. It is assumed without loss of generality that only one item type flows on each link and that the input and output flows to/from node j, represented by column vectors $q_{\bullet j}$ and $q_{j\bullet}$ respectively, are related by: $q_{\bullet j} = \Pi_j\, q_{j\bullet}$, where Π_j is a matrix of constant coefficients that depends on the production technology. (This matrix is a column vector for merge-nodes and a scalar for ordinary nodes.) It is also assumed that the optimum steady-state inventories by item type at j are given by known functions of the output flows: $K_{\bullet j}(q_{j\bullet})$. If these functions are linear (or are linearized) then the ACT equations are a superposition of the linear-homogeneous equations for each commodity, considered separately. Therefore, it follows from the superposition principle, that the whole system will be stable (reliable, monotone, bounded) under the ACT policy if all the trees are stable (reliable, monotone, bounded). The stability (reliability, monotonicity, boundedness) of the trees can be checked as explained above. It is also possible, although this is not done here, to extend the cost-estimation results of Chapter 6 to networks, and to optimize the $K_{\bullet j}$ functions, both, from "user-optimal" and JIT standpoints.

7.2 Application issues

These notes have assumed throughout that all the suppliers make decisions at the same discrete times. Although this may appear on the surface to be rather restrictive, it should be stressed that it is not. Synchronicity on the lattice does not require synchronicity in real time. Only that suppliers should act with the same frequency; e.g., weekly. For example, if the first supplier makes its decisions at the open of business on Mondays and supplier two on Tuesdays, one should simply designate these moments as being the points on the lattice, and then define the stencils and ordering rules of the policies accordingly. Of course, a network of this type might require different stencils for different suppliers, but the resulting problem is still in the family of (inhomogeneous) problems that have already been addressed in these notes.

The notes have not examined systems of suppliers that act with different frequencies, but the results can often be applied to these cases too; e.g., when a chain is composed of a few sub-chains with specific frequencies so that the stability of the sub-chains guarantees the stability of the system.

The notes have also assumed that the item number variable is continuous, when in many real applications items are discrete. Obviously, this is not a problem for systems where orders include many items but it should be emphasized that the continuity assumption is immaterial, even if orders are small, for flexible commitment systems and for JIT systems. (The systems studied in Sec. 6.) This is true because flexible commitment systems work on bounds that can be continuous, and JIT procedures produce integer outputs for integer inputs.

Finally note that these notes have assumed perfect reliability in communications and execution, and this cannot be expected in practice. Therefore, an understanding of the occasional system failures and recoveries arising in mildly unreliable systems should also be developed, e.g., when the M_j are chosen to be large, but not equal to the one-hundred[th] percentile of the random process times, or when some items are defective. Our initial research on this subject shows that mildly unreliable systems designed to fail infrequently and to be strongly stable when operating normally, continue to be strongly stable despite the failures. A detailed analysis of mildly unreliable systems including cost estimation is beyond the scope of these notes, however, and is left for future work.

References

Blackburn, J. D. (1991) The quick response movement in the apparel industry: a case study in time-compressing supply chains, in Time-based Competition: The Next Battleground in American Manufacturing, Irwin, Homewood, IL, Chapter 11.

Blinder, A.S. (1986). Can the production smoothing model of inventory behavior be saved?, Quaterly Journal of Economics, **101**, 431-53.

Buffa, E.S. and J.G. Miller (1979). Production- Inventory Systems: Planning and Control, Richard D. Irwin Inc., Illinois.

Chen, F., Z. Drevner, J.K. Ryan and D. Simchi-Levi (2000). Quantifying the Bullwhip Effect in a Simple Supply Chain: The Impact of Forecasting, Lead Times and Information, Management Science, **46**(3), 436-443.

Courant, R. and D. Hilbert (1953) Methods of mathematical physics (Volume I) Wiley, New York, N.Y.

Daganzo, C. F. (1993) The cell-transmission model: A dynamic representation of highway traffic consistent with the hydrodynamic theory, Institute of Transportation Studies, Research Report, UCB-ITS-RR-93-7, Univ. of California, Berkeley, CA; abbreviated in Trans. Res., **28B**(4), 269-287.

Daganzo, C. F. (1994) The cell-transmission model. Part II: network traffic, PATH working paper UCB-ITS-PWP-94-12, Univ. of California, Berkeley, CA; abbreviated in Trans. Res., **29B**(2), 79-94.

Daganzo, C. F. (1995) A finite difference approximation of the kinematic wave model of traffic flow, Trans. Res. **29B**(4), 261-276.

Daganzo, C. F. (1997) A simple traffic analysis procedure, ITS Working Paper, UCB-ITS-WP-97-4; abbreviated in Networks and Spatial Economics **1**, 77-101 (2001).

Daganzo, C.F. (1999) Logistics systems analysis (3rd edition), Springer, Heidelberg, Germany.

Erera, A. (2001) Private communications.

Forrester, J.W. (1961) Industrial Dynamics , MIT press, and John Wiley and Sons, Inc., New York.

Gallego, G. and O. Ozer (2001), Integrating Replenishment Decisions with Advance Demand Information, Management Science, **40**, 1678-1689.

Garabedian, P. R. (1986) Partial differential equations (2nd edition), Chelsea, New York, N.Y.

Gazis, D. C. and R. B. Potts (1965), The over-saturated intersection, Proc. 2nd Int. Symp. on the Theory of Road Traffic Flow, (J. Almond, editor), pp. 221-237, OECD, Paris, France.

Goodwin, J., S. Franklin (1994), The Beer Distribution Game: Using Simulation to Teach Systems Thinking, Journal of Management Development, **13**(8), 7-15.

Graves, S.C. (1999). A Single-Item Inventory Model for a Nonstationary Demand Process, Manufacturing & Service Operations Management, 1(1).

Hariharan, R. and P. Zipkin (1995). Customer-order Information, Leadtimes and Inventories, Management Science, 41, 1599-1607.

Holt, C.C., Modigliani, F., Muth, J. and Simon, H.A. (1960). Planning Production, Inventories and Work Force, Prentice Hall.

Hurdle, V. F. and Son, B. (2000) Road test of a freeway model, Trans. Res. 34A, 537-564.

Kahn, J.A. (1987). Inventories and the volatility of production. American Economic Review, 77, 667-79.

Karaesman, F., J.A. Buzacott and Y. Dallery (2002). Integrating advance order information in make-to-stock production systems, IIE Transactions, 34, 649-62.

Lawson, T., D. Lovell and C. F. Daganzo (1997) Using the input-output diagram to determine the spatial and temporal extent of a queue upstream of a bottleneck, Trans. Res. Rec. 1572, pp. 140-147.

Lax, P. D. (1973) Hyperbolic systems of conservation laws and the mathematical theory of shockwaves, SIAM Regional Conference Series in Applied Mathematics. J. W. Arrowsmith Ltd., Bristol, U.K.

Lebacque, J. P. (1993) Les modèles macroscopiques de traffic, Annales de Ponts (3rd trim) 67, 28-45.

LeVeque, R. J. (1992) Numerical methods for conservation laws, (2nd edition), Birkhauser-Verlag, Boston, MA.

Lee, H., V. Padmanabhan, S. Whang (1997a), The Bullwhip Effect in Supply Chains, Sloan Management Review, Spring, 93-102.

Lee, H., V. Padmanabhan, S. Whang (1997b), Information Distortion in a Supply Chain: The Bullwhip Effect, Management Science, 43(4), 546-558.

Linsley, R. K. and J. B. Franzini (1955) Elements of hydraulic engineering, McGraw-Hill, New York, N.Y.

Lighthill, M.J. and G.B. Whitham (1955), On kinematic waves. I Flow movement in long rivers. II A theory of traffic flow on long crowded roads, Proc. Roy. Soc. A, 229, 281-345.

Magee, J. and Boodman, D. (1967) Production Planning and Inventory Control, (2nd edition) McGraw-Hill, New York, N.Y.

Makigami, Y., G. F. Newell, and R. Rothery (1971), Three-dimensional representation of traffic flow, Trans. Sci. 5, 302-313.

Metters, R. (1997), Quantifying the Bullwhip Effect in Supply Chains, Journal of Operations Management, 15, 89-100.

Moskowitz, K. (1954) Waiting for a gap in a traffic stream, Proc. Highway Res. Board 33, 385-395.

Naish, H.F. (1994). Production Smoothing in the Linear Quadratic Inventory Model, The Economic Journal, 104, Issue 425, 864-75.

Newell, G. F. (1971) Applications of queueing theory, Chapman Hall, London.

Newell, G. F. (1993), A simplified theory of kinematic waves in highway traffic. I general theory, II queuing at freeway bottlenecks, III multi-destination flows, Trans. Res. 27B, 281-313.

Peterson, R. and E. A. Silver (1979) Decision systems for inventory management and production planning, Wiley, New York, N.Y.

Ramey , V.A. (1991) Nonconvex costs and the behavior of inventories, Journal of Political Economy, **99**, 306-34.

Richards, P. I. (1956) Shockwaves on the highway, Opns. Res. **4**, 42-51.

Ryan, J. K. (1997) Analysis of inventory models with limited demand information, Ph.D. thesis, IEMS Dept., Northwestern University, Evanston, IL.

Simchi-Levi, D., Kaminsky, P. and Simchi-Levi, E. (2000) Designing and managing the supply chain, McGraw-Hill, New York, N.Y.

Stengel, R. F. (1994) Optimal control and estimation, Dover, New York, N.Y.

Sterman, J.D. (1989), Modeling Managerial Behavior: Misperceptions of Feedback in a Dynamic Decision-Making Experiment, Management Science, **35**(3), 321-339.

Wardrop, J. G. (1952) Some theoretical aspects of road traffic research, Proc. Inst. Civ. Eng. Part II **1**(2), 325-362; Discussion, 362-378.

White, J., S. Garside and J. Whitaker (1998) A verification of a cell-type transmission model, World Conference on Transportation Research, Antwerp, Belgium.

Whitham, G. B. (1974) Linear and non-linear waves, Wiley, New York, N.Y.

Zipkin, P. H. (2000) Foundations of inventory management, McGraw-Hill, New York, N.Y.

Appendix A: Stability via Control Theory

This appendix shows that a control theory treatment of equation (4.6) yields the same results of the text. A good introduction to control theory, including the background necessary to follow this appendix, is given in Stengel (1994). In the control theory lingo, Equation (4.6) is an "open loop, linear system with constant coefficients". These systems are conventionally treated with the z-transform and then analyzed in "frequency-domain".

If we use $q_j(z)$ for the z-transform of $\{..., Q_{j,n}, Q_{j,n+1}, ...\}$ and apply the transform to both sides of (4.6), assuming that the boundary conditions are well-posed and such that $Q_{j,n} = 0$ if $n \leq 0$, then (4.6) becomes:

$$q_j(z) = q_{j-1}(z)T(z), \tag{A1}$$

where $T(z)$ is the following "transfer function":

$$T(z) = (\beta_{-A}z^A + \beta_{1-A}z^{A-1} + ...)/(z-\alpha). \tag{A2}$$

Equation (A1) is the frequency domain expression of (4.6). The expression is more convenient than (4.6) because it can be iterated for increasing j, so that the behavior of a supplier can be directly related to the behavior of the input data; i.e., we can write:

$$q_j(z) = q_0(z)T(z)^j. \tag{A3}$$

It is known from control theory that for the time-series $\{..., Q_{j,n}, Q_{j,n+1}, ...\}$ to be bounded whenever its direct input $\{..., Q_{j-1,n}, Q_{j-1,n+1}, ...\}$ is bounded, i.e., for the underlying policy to be "proper", the poles of the transfer function must be in the unit circle. Consideration of (A2) shows that this happens if and only if $|\alpha| \leq 1$. This result is consistent with the findings of Sec. 3.1.

Control theory books are less explicit about the stability of a system such as (4.6) when both n and j can vary, in particular when one considers the case where $j \to \infty$. Nonetheless, a result can be derived as follows.

First write the expression for $Q_{j,n}$ for some input data $Q_{0,n}$ by applying the z-transform inversion formula to (A3). The result is:

$$Q_{j,n} = \frac{1}{2\pi i} \oint T(z)^j z^{n-1} q_0(z) dz, \tag{A4}$$

where the path of integration can be any closed curve enclosing all the poles of T and q_0. We choose the path of integration to be the unit circle. Next, we check what must happen to $T(z)$ for (A4) to remain bounded as $j \to \infty$, for any customer data, $q_0(z)$.

Note that if the modulus of $T(z)$ had a maximum greater than 1 along the unit circle for some $z = z^*$, then for sufficiently large j, the integrand of (A4) would be much larger in a neighborhood of z^* than elsewhere on the unit circle, and the integral could be evaluated by considering only this neighborhood. Since z and $q_0(z)$ are approximately constant in such a neighborhood, we see from (A4) that the modulus of this result would increase exponentially with j with an amplification factor, $|T(z^*)|$. Thus, the system would be unstable. The same logic, applied in the reverse, reveals that for (A4) to have a non-diverging and non-zero solution (i.e., to be stable), the modulus of the transfer function would have to reach a *global* maximum of 1 (for $z = 1$), along the unit circle. This condition turns out to be equivalent to the results of Sec. 4.2, as explained below.

Since the transfer function is evaluated on the unit circle, we can replace z in (A2) by $\exp(-\omega i)$, with $\omega \in [-\pi, \pi]$, and write:

$$T(\exp(-\omega i)) = \sum_{l=-A}^{\infty} \beta_l \exp(l\omega i) / [\exp(-\omega i) - \alpha]$$

$$= \exp(\omega i) \sum_{l=-A}^{\infty} \beta_l \exp(l\omega i) / [1 - \alpha\exp(\omega i)].$$

Therefore, the modulus of T along the unit circle is:

$$|T(\exp(-\omega i))| = |\exp(\omega i)| \left| \sum_{l=-A}^{\infty} \beta_l \exp(l\omega i) / [1 - \alpha\exp(\omega i)] \right|$$

$$= \left| \sum_{l=-A}^{\infty} \beta_l \exp(l\omega i) / [1 - \alpha\exp(\omega i)] \right|,$$

which coincides with the modulus of $\xi(\omega)$, as per Equation (4.8) of the text. The equality, $|T(\exp(-\omega i))| = |\xi(\omega)|$, is the connection between control theory and Sec. 4.2.

The equality implies two things: (i) that the Von Neumann stability condition (4.9) is equivalent to the control theory condition $|T(z)| \leq 1$, and (ii) that the existence condition (4.7) is equivalent to the control theory condition that the modulus of $T(z)$ should have a *local* maximum of 1 for $z = 1$. Hence, both approaches yield the same stability results.

For unstable systems, the Von Neumann amplification factor introduced in the text, $|\xi^*|$, matches the amplification factor found in this appendix, $|T(z^*)|$. Furthermore, consideration of the asymptotic structure of (A4) reveals that the oscillation periods predicted by both methods also coincide. As expected, the two methods yield consistent results in the unstable case too.

Appendix B: Kinematic Wave Theory Revisited

This appendix contains an unconventional introduction to kinematic wave (KW) theory and proves the results in Daganzo (1997) that were cited in the body of the monograph. Based on Section 2 of this reference, the appendix is written in the context of traffic flow and is self-contained. It uses the notation of the reference, which is similar but not identical to that used in the monograph. The focus of analysis is a queued but homogeneous freeway section between two detectors (U-upstream and D-downstream). The method predicts the N-curve at "U" from that at "D". The results are developed assuming that curve N_D is piecewise linear (as is typically the case in applications), and then extended at the end of the appendix to the general case.

B.1 Preliminaries.

N-**curves** - The vehicle number function $N(t, x)$, originally proposed in Moskowitz (1965), later refined in Makigami et al (1971) and more recently introduced to kinematic wave (KW) theory in Newell (1993), shall be used to summarize the traffic stream features of interest. Moskowitz's function is most easily described in terms of imaginary numbered labels, n, that are carried by vehicles. It is assumed that there is no passing, and that the labels have been numbered consecutively at time $t = 0$, increasing in unit increments in the upstream direction along the line of cars. If traffic flows in the direction of increasing x, the label at a point in space-time, $n = N(t, x)$, increases with t and decreases with x. [Function $N(t, x)$ is the traffic version of the $u(x, t)$ function used in the body of the monograph. The only difference is that the direction of flow in traffic models is opposite to the direction assumed in the monograph; hence $u(-x, t) = N(t, x)$.]

Note that a particular Moskowitz function describes a geometric surface in (t, x, n) space. The intersection of this surface and the plane $x = x'$, corresponding to a specific location x', yields a (t, n) curve that will be denoted by a capital letter (usually "N") subscripted by an identifier of the location; e.g., $N_{x'}$. The capital letter represents the particular geometric surface (traffic instance) from which the curve comes. When a location is identified by means of a subscript, e.g., x_p , the subscript may be used to identify the corresponding (t, n) curve, e.g., N_p.

Tolerances - The appendix will show that if N_D and N'_D are two input data curves within a tolerance ε (vehicles) of each other, then the output curves at any upstream location N_U and N'_U will also be within the same tolerance. That is,

$$\left\| N_D - N'_D \right\| \le \varepsilon \quad \Rightarrow \quad \left\| N_U - N'_U \right\| \le \varepsilon . \tag{B1}$$

The vertical bars in (B1) signify the maximum absolute value over time. [By selecting the two input curves in a convenient way, it will be shown at the end of this appendix that the maximum vehicular accumulation between evenly spaced detectors cannot increase in the upstream direction. This proves the stringent stability condition mentioned in the body of the monograph; i.e., that $sup\{u_j(t)-u_{j-1}(t)\}$ is non-increasing in j.]

B.2 The KW Theory Revisited.

This subsection presents a simple method for predicting N_U from N_D. The procedure is based on three postulates equivalent to those of KW theory. It will be described in steps, one postulate at a time.

Postulate 1: Reproducibility of stationary conditions inside a queue. If curve N_D becomes straight with slope q, and remains so as time advances, then curve N_U should become parallel to it and remain to the left of N_D by an amount $\tau(q)$. Alternatively, curve N_U should stabilize $m(q) = q\tau(q)$ vehicle positions above curve N_D . ∎

It is assumed that the observed flow is strictly less than the maximum possible, q_{max} , and that the section is queued. We assume that postulate 1 holds for any pair of locations x_i, x_j $(x_i < x_j)$ inside the queue and therefore that the translations at consecutive locations are additive; i.e., that $m_{ij}(q) + m_{jk}(q) = m_{ik}(q)$. From now on the location-specific subscripts may be omitted when there is no room for confusion. The postulate can be used by itself to study bottlenecks with constant capacity, even if the sections are inhomogeneous (Lawson et al, 1997).

For the general case [with time-dependent capacity] more assumptions are needed. It will be assumed that the highway section is homogeneous, in the sense that the stationary accumulation between "D" or "U" and any intermediate location "M" is proportional to the length of the subsection; i.e., if $(x_D - x_M) = \alpha(x_D - x_U)$ for $0 < \alpha < 1$, then $m_{DM}(q) = \alpha m_{DU}(q)$ and $m_{MU}(q) = (1-\alpha)m_{DU}(q)$ for all q. This means that accumulations and trip times should be evenly distributed over the segment for all flows. Clearly, homogeneity allows us to write all the $m_{x,x'}(q)$ of a highway in terms of the normalized relation between m and q that holds for a segment of unit length, $K(q)$; i.e., $m_{x,x'}(q) = (x-x')K(q)$. Our objective is finding a set of rules [consistent with KW theory] that will allow us to predict N_U from N_D if $m_{DU}(q)$ is given.

First, let us extend postulate 1 to the time-dependent case. We shall assume that N_D is piecewise linear, changing from (steady) state "i" to state "$i+1$" at time t_i. The original postulate indicates that if there is a transition between two lasting stationary states at detector D, marked by a change in the slope of N_D from q_1 to q_2, the same stationary states should also arise at the upstream detector. It is now further assumed that the transitions between neighboring states occur rapidly and propagate upstream as a wave. Therefore, we have:

Postulate 1 (Time-dependent reproducibility). Lasting stationary states are reproduced upstream. Furthermore, transitions between neighboring states propagate sharply as a wave. ∎

The procedure implied by this postulate is illustrated in figure B1, for the simple case when there is only one transition, between states "1" and "2". Part "a" of the figure shows that the construction of N_U is easy, insofar as the two segments of curve N_U must be at specific separations from the corresponding segments of N_D.

We note as an aside that the correctness of a result can be verified at a glance (without any numerical calculations) if one uses the diagram on part "b" of the figure. This diagram contains both, an $m(q)$ relation and a companion curve of $\tau(q)$ vs. $m(q)$, where q is the slope of the ray passing through the origin. Curve $m(q)$ plays the role of the so-called "fundamental diagram" of KW theory. [And the same role as the $K(q)$ curve in the supply chain problem.] The companion curve of m vs. τ is useful because if the diagrams of parts "a" and "b" have been drawn with the proper scale then the horizontal and vertical separation between any two parallel portions of the N-curves that correspond to the same state should be equal to the coordinates of the given state on the $m(\tau)$ curve. Furthermore, the slope of an N-curve should be equal to the slope of the line that connects the given state on the $m(\tau)$ curve with the origin. These properties can be used to verify the "correctness" of a solution. Let us now return to part "a" of the figure.

Note from the geometry of the picture that the transition point "C" from the first segment to the second must occur with a precise delay, w_{12}, that should only be a function of the two transition states. More specifically, note from the slopes of the sides of triangle (ABC) that this delay can be written as:

$$w_{12} = -[m_1 - m_2]/[q_1 - q_2] \qquad (B2)$$

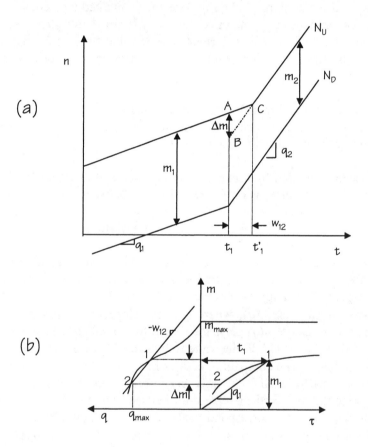

Figure B1 Steady states and the propagation of changes

and that as a result w_{12} will be positive for any pair of states if $m(q)$ decreases. A positive w means that information (causation) travels in the upstream direction, as one would expect inside queues. A graphical interpretation of (B2) is possible from the fundamental diagram of Fig. B1b; namely, that the negative slope of a line joining two states on the $m(q)$ plot is the delay in the propagation of information. (This delay is the shockwave trip time of KW theory.)

If N_D changes stationary state more than once and the upstream transition times calculated with (B2), $t'_i = t_i + w_{i,i+1}$, satisfy:

$$t'_i < t'_{i+1}, \quad \text{for all } i, \quad \text{where } t'_i = t_i + w_{i,i+1}, \tag{B3}$$

then curve N_U can be obtained by applying the graphical procedure of Fig. B1 to all the states and the result will contain all the original states with breaks at the t'_i. The time $(t'_{i+1} - t'_i)$ is the duration of steady state $i+1$ upstream.

In what follows it will be convenient to describe the performance of the algorithm we are looking for by a set of "upstream" operators $U = \{U_s\}$, where the subscript "s" refers to the segment length, s. That is, U_sN will denote the result of the algorithm, when applied to a generic curve "N" at the downstream end of a length-s segment. When referring to a specific highway segment, U will be subscripted by two variables that identify the end points of the segment (instead of the single variable "length") with the downstream identifier placed first. With this convention the output of the algorithm for a given downstream curve and particular highway segment can be compactly expressed as $N_U = U_{DU}N_D$. Note that when the two identifiers are coordinates then $U_{x,x'} = U_{x-x'}$.

If the input data vary so slowly that (B3) is satisfied, then the procedure just described is the "upstream operator." Otherwise, modifications are needed. The modifications we seek should satisfy the following composition rule:

Postulate 2 (Transitivity). If $s = s' + s''$, then $U_s = U_{s'}U_{s''}$. ∎

This means that if N_U is the curve that is obtained from N_D using relationship $m_{DU}(q)$, then N_U should also be the curve that is obtained in two steps: (i) by applying the procedure to curve N_D with relationship $m_{DM}(q)$, and (ii) repeating the process with the resulting curve (N_M) and relationship $m_{MU}(q)$. The postulate also implies that a highway section can be divided into many parts and studied sequentially.

The reader is encouraged to verify that the procedure as it currently stands (for cases where (B3) holds) is divisible and satisfies this postulate; e.g., that the breaks in the N-curve at any intermediate position that is $\alpha 100\%$ of the way toward the upstream detector occur with a delay αw_{12}. Postulate 2 is now used to break the procedure into steps for cases where (B3) does not hold.

We first look for an intermediate location "M_1" with the largest possible value of the interpolation parameter α, for which (B4a), below holds:

$$t'_i \leq t'_{i+1}, \quad \text{for all } i, \quad \text{where } t'_i = t_i + \alpha w_{i,i+1}. \tag{B4a}$$

Note that all the states i for which $t'_{i-1} = t'_i$ are observed for zero time at location "M_1". Thus, they have vanished. Next, we use the transitivity postulate to find the solution for locations upstream of M_1. We simply treat these locations as if M_1 was the location of the downstream data. To express this idea as a recursion it is convenient to rewrite (B4a) as:

$$t'_i \leq t'_j, \text{ for all } (i,j) \text{ such that } i < j, \text{ where } t'_i = t_i + \alpha w_{i,i+1}, \tag{B4b}$$

and introduce S_k for the set of surviving states at location M_k after the kth iteration ($k = 1$, for now). Since the straight lines obtained by shifting the segments of the N-curve at location M_k are the same as those obtained by shifting the original (surviving) segments from the N-curve at location "D", we can simply choose α_{k+1} as the maximum value of α ($\alpha \leq 1$) that satisfies:

$$t'_i \leq t'_j, \text{ for all } i,j \in S_k \text{ such that } i < j, \text{ where } t'_i = t_i + \alpha w_{i,i+1}. \tag{B5}$$

The recursive process terminates when (B5) is satisfied for $\alpha = 1$. This algorithm can now be applied to any data set, but for reasons about to be presented it is not yet the final product. The current version of the algorithm will be named "A", and its results expressed by $N_U = A_{DU} N_D$.

The procedure is particularly quick when done by hand, and this can help in the interpretation of data. Consider as an illustration Fig. B2, which shows the result when the downstream state changes from "1" to "3" with a brief sojourn in state "2", for the $m(q)$ relation shown on the top left corner. The figure also displays the N-curve for a detector "M" which is halfway between "U" and "D" ($\alpha = 0.5$).

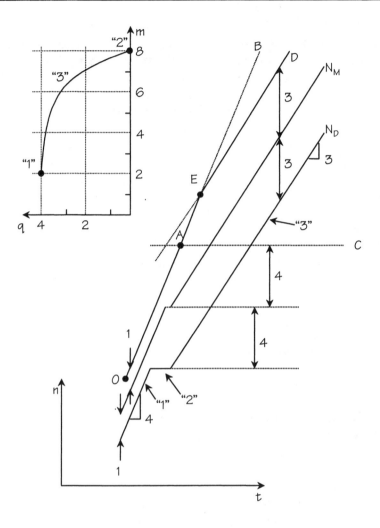

Figure B2 Disappearance of a state

The figure shows that the shifted lines corresponding to the three linear segments of N_D (lines OAB, AC and ED) do not intersect in the order required by (B3) because line ED is beyond the apex of angle OAC. However, if the same construction is repeated for location "M" by cutting the three shifts in half then the three lines intersect in the proper way, as shown. We see at a glance that the duration of state "2" is reduced in going from "D" to "M", and that state "2" would be completely eliminated farther upstream, somewhere between "M" and "U"; i.e., that $0.5 < \alpha_1 < 1$. Note that we do not need to find α_1 to obtain N_U, since our knowledge that only states "1" and "3" survive the trip to location "U" already allows us to use (B5). That is, the final solution--line OAED--is simply obtained by connecting the original translations of the two surviving segments. In cases with more state transitions and longer separations between detectors more steps may be needed to determine which states are eliminated but procedure "A" remains simple.

The third and final postulate of the proposed theory for the description of queues involves the idea of "stability". The proposed algorithm does not rule out the possibility that an infinitesimal change in N_D could trigger a finite change in N_U, and we wish to exclude such "unstable" solutions from the set of possibilities. In particular, we specify that if a continuum of transition states of infinitesimal duration are introduced at every corner of N_D, i.e., we smooth the corners of N_D, then the final solution should not be affected by the smoothing. We also require this to be true for any inter-mediate solution. In other words, if S denotes the operator that smoothes the corners, we assume that $U_s = U_s S$ for all s; i.e.:

Postulate 3 (Stability). The operators U_s and S commute. ∎

Figure B3 is used to illustrate these ideas. Part (a) shows by means of thick solid lines a construction for N_U similar to that of Fig. B2, with algorithm "A", when a transition from state "1" to state "2" has occurred at "D". If we imagine that the transition at point V has occurred by way of an infinitesimally quick sojourn through intermediate state "k", we see that this state cannot appear into the solution because if we shift the imaginary line passing through "V" corresponding to this state, the resulting line (labeled L_k in the figure) does not intersect our test N_U curve. Thus, the test curve is not destabilized by "k". Further consideration shows that the state will not enter into the solution as long as its corresponding point "k" on the (q, m)-plane is below or on the chord joining states "1" and "2" on such plane; see figure. Clearly, the higher this point is, the larger the shift imparted to L_k. It turns out that if the point is on the chord, then line L_k passes through the vertex of N_U. However, states that lie above the chord, such as k', would enter the solution as shown by line $L_{k'}$ and they would destabilize the solution.

If instead of an increase in flow, we had experienced a decrease, then we see from the geometry that algorithm "A" introduces intermediate states into the solution if they experience a small shift. They will appear in the solution if they lie below the chord. Any solution that can be modified by means of an infinitesimal perturbation could not be expected to arise in real life and should be ruled out. Thus, algorithm "A" needs to be modified and this is done below. The desired effect is achieved by treating each change, i, in the slope of N_D as being gradual and then determining which sequence of intermediate states appears immediately upstream; this will be called the "stable transition sequence".

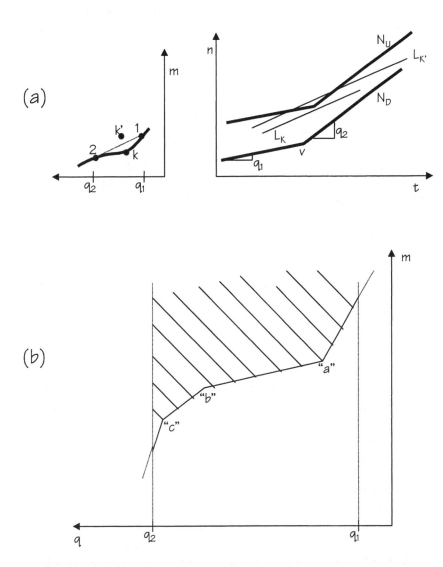

Figure B3 Stable and unstable transitions

The logic used earlier on part (a) of the figure reveals that a proposed transition involving a particular sequence of intermediate states and an *increase* in flow is stable if and only if the portion of the $m(q)$ curve joining any two states in the sequence [such as "1" and "2" in part(a) of the figure] does not protrude above the chord joining the two states on the (q, m)-plane. For piecewise linear $m(q)$ relations as in Fig. B3b the relevant solution should be the highest possible sequence of chords that can be formed from $m(q)$. The stable break-points are vertices of the convex hull of the unshaded portion of Fig. B3b. Since the m-value for each stable break-point is as high as possible, it should be clear that: (i) this procedure will also connect the two original segments of the N_U-curve by the highest possible arc that can be constructed by a succession of intermediate states, and (ii) that if the $m(q)$ curve is convex only its extreme points propagate into the solution--the original jump is then said to be "stable." (Stable jumps correspond to "shocks" in KW theory.)

If the transition involves a reduction in flow, then the results are reversed. One would look for the convex hull of the *shaded* area, and would find that the stable transition for N_U is achieved by the *lowest* possible arc of intermediate states. The original jump would be stable if the $m(q)$ curve is *concave*.

Note that in both cases, whether there is an increase or a decrease in flow, the corner of N_U is spanned by an arc of new states that is as far away from the original corner as possible; i.e. in all cases, corners are smoothed as much as possible. Furthermore, in the piecewise linear case only break-points of the $m(q)$ curve can appear as new intermediate states. Obviously, we can imagine that these are the only states actually introduced by S, and this simplification allows us to devise a simple stable procedure.

Algorithm "U"

Let x_D and x_U denote the positions of the downstream and upstream detectors, and x_M the position of an intermediate trial location such that $x_U \le x_M \le x_D$. The intermediate location represents the most upstream location at which an N-curve, N_M, is known. The algorithm starts with $x_M = x_D$ and then reduces x_M iteratively until $x_M = x_U$. Each iteration has two steps: "smoothing" and "shifting":

Step 1: Smoothing. Smooth N_M by introducing the necessary intermediate states at its corners as described above. The result is denoted SN_M.

Step 2: Shifting. Find the most upstream location x^*, $x_M \ge x^* \ge x_U$, for which the shift imparted to the segments of SN_M with algorithm A does not eliminate any states. (This ensures that all the intermediate states are stable.) The resulting curve is called N^*. If $x^* = x_U$, then $N_U = N^*$ and the procedure ends. Otherwise, set $x_M = x^*$, $N_M = N^*$ and repeat.

B.3 Properties of the procedure.

This section examines the effect that errors in the input data N_D have on the solution. It will be shown that the maximum error in the solution cannot exceed the maximum error in the data. [It will also be shown that this establishes the stringent stability property used in the body of this monograph and that the result holds for non-piecewise linear data curves.]

Let us first consider the effect of a differential operator $dU = U_{dx}$ on two similar, piecewise linear data curves N and N'. We are interested in determining the change in the maximum vertical separation between the curves that is induced by the operation.

In the neighborhood of the location where this maximum change takes place, one or both of the curves will bend; e.g., as shown on Fig. B4. The dotted lines on this figure represent the upstream curves [after the application of dU.]. It should be clear from the geometry of the figure that at the time t^* where the separation is at a maximum, the smoothed lines SN and SN' must share a common flow q^* at that time. (Otherwise their separation would be changing at $t = t^*$, which is not possible.)

We then see from the rules of Fig. B3 and the present geometry that the separation between either of the lines, e.g., N, and an intermediate data line N^* with slope q^* (also shown in the figure) cannot increase [with the application of dU] because otherwise there is a contradiction. That is, if the separation between dUN^* and dUN was larger than the separation between N^* and N, then the shifted line corresponding to state q^* of curve N would intersect dUN (since the shift imparted to the line with slope q^* is the same as that imparted to N^*). But this is not allowed by the rules of Fig. B3.

Since neither of the solution lines can drift away from the intermediate line, it must be true that $\| dUN - dUN' \| \le \| N - N' \|$. Clearly now, since U is transitive, it follows that:

$$\| U_s N - U_s N' \| \le \| N - N' \| \qquad \text{for all } s, N \text{ and } N'. \qquad (B6)$$

Thus, U_s is a (non-strict) contraction mapping in the space of N-curves.

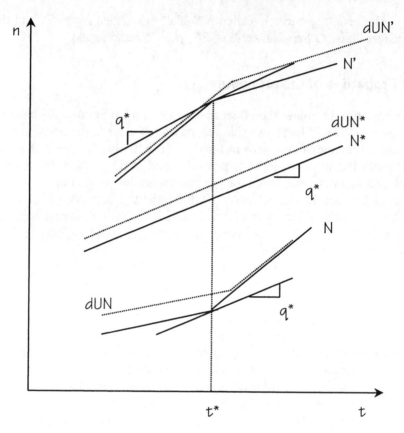

Figure B4 The contraction property

Stringent stability result: If the detectors on a freeway are evenly spaced s distance units apart, and we use in (B6) the KW curves for any two adjoining detectors, $N = N_i$ and $N' = N_{i+1}$, then (B6) expresses a recursion for the maximum accumulation between successive pairs of detectors. It says that the maximum accumulation between detectors [suppliers] cannot increase. [This is the stringent stability result mentioned in the body of this monograph.]

General input data: The results of this appendix also apply to non-piecewise linear data, provided that the input curve, N_D, can be expressed as the limit of a sequence of piecewise linear input curves $\{N_D^{(i)}\}$ [under the metric defined by $\|\cdot\|$.] In view of (B6), it should be clear that since

$\{N_D^{(i)}\}$ converges to an N-curve then the sequence of solutions $\{N_U^{(i)}\} = \{U_sN_D^{(i)}\}$ also converges to a curve, N_U, which is the solution. This is true for all s. Obviously then, the KW solution exists and is unique. Furthermore, since (B6) and the stringent stability result are satisfied by all the members of the sequence, they are also satisfied by the solution.

Printing and Binding: Strauss GmbH, Mörlenbach

Lecture Notes in Economics and Mathematical Systems

For information about Vols. 1–429
please contact your bookseller or Springer-Verlag

Vol. 475: L. Kaas, Dynamic Macroeconomics with Imperfect Competition. XI, 155 pages. 1999.

Vol. 476: R. Demel, Fiscal Policy, Public Debt and the Term Structure of Interest Rates. X, 279 pages. 1999.

Vol. 477: M. Théra, R. Tichatschke (Eds.), Ill-posed Variational Problems and Regularization Techniques. VIII, 274 pages. 1999.

Vol. 478: S. Hartmann, Project Scheduling under Limited Resources. XII, 221 pages. 1999.

Vol. 479: L. v. Thadden, Money, Inflation, and Capital Formation. IX, 192 pages. 1999.

Vol. 480: M. Grazia Speranza, P. Stähly (Eds.), New Trends in Distribution Logistics. X, 336 pages. 1999.

Vol. 481: V. H. Nguyen, J. J. Strodiot, P. Tossings (Eds.). Optimation. IX, 498 pages. 2000.

Vol. 482: W. B. Zhang, A Theory of International Trade. XI, 192 pages. 2000.

Vol. 483: M. Königstein, Equity, Efficiency and Evolutionary Stability in Bargaining Games with Joint Production. XII, 197 pages. 2000.

Vol. 484: D. D. Gatti, M. Gallegati, A. Kirman, Interaction and Market Structure. VI, 298 pages. 2000.

Vol. 485: A. Garnaev, Search Games and Other Applications of Game Theory. VIII, 145 pages. 2000.

Vol. 486: M. Neugart, Nonlinear Labor Market Dynamics. X, 175 pages. 2000.

Vol. 487: Y. Y. Haimes, R. E. Steuer (Eds.), Research and Practice in Multiple Criteria Decision Making. XVII, 553 pages. 2000.

Vol. 488: B. Schmolck, Ommitted Variable Tests and Dynamic Specification. X, 144 pages. 2000.

Vol. 489: T. Steger, Transitional Dynamics and Economic Growth in Developing Countries. VIII, 151 pages. 2000.

Vol. 490: S. Minner, Strategic Safety Stocks in Supply Chains. XI, 214 pages. 2000.

Vol. 491: M. Ehrgott, Multicriteria Optimization. VIII, 242 pages. 2000.

Vol. 492: T. Phan Huy, Constraint Propagation in Flexible Manufacturing. IX, 258 pages. 2000.

Vol. 493: J. Zhu, Modular Pricing of Options. X, 170 pages. 2000.

Vol. 494: D. Franzen, Design of Master Agreements for OTC Derivatives. VIII, 175 pages. 2001.

Vol. 495: I Konnov, Combined Relaxation Methods for Variational Inequalities. XI, 181 pages. 2001.

Vol. 496: P. Weiß, Unemployment in Open Economies. XII, 226 pages. 2001.

Vol. 497: J. Inkmann, Conditional Moment Estimation of Nonlinear Equation Systems. VIII, 214 pages. 2001.

Vol. 498: M. Reutter, A Macroeconomic Model of West German Unemployment. X, 125 pages. 2001.

Vol. 499: A. Casajus, Focal Points in Framed Games. XI, 131 pages. 2001.

Vol. 500: F. Nardini, Technical Progress and Economic Growth. XVII, 191 pages. 2001.

Vol. 501: M. Fleischmann, Quantitative Models for Reverse Logistics. XI, 181 pages. 2001.

Vol. 502: N. Hadjisavvas, J. E. Martínez-Legaz, J.-P. Penot (Eds.), Generalized Convexity and Generalized Monotonicity. IX, 410 pages. 2001.

Vol. 503: A. Kirman, J.-B. Zimmermann (Eds.), Economics with Heterogenous Interacting Agents. VII, 343 pages. 2001.

Vol. 504: P.-Y. Moix (Ed.),The Measurement of Market Risk. XI, 272 pages. 2001.

Vol. 505: S. Voß, J. R. Daduna (Eds.), Computer-Aided Scheduling of Public Transport. XI, 466 pages. 2001.

Vol. 506: B. P. Kellerhals, Financial Pricing Models in Continuous Time and Kalman Filtering. XIV, 247 pages. 2001.

Vol. 507: M. Koksalan, S. Zionts, Multiple Criteria Decision Making in the New Millenium. XII, 481 pages. 2001.

Vol. 508: K. Neumann, C. Schwindt, J. Zimmermann, Project Scheduling with Time Windows and Scarce Resources. XI, 335 pages. 2002.

Vol. 509: D. Hornung, Investment, R&D, and Long-Run Growth. XVI, 194 pages. 2002.

Vol. 510: A. S. Tangian, Constructing and Applying Objective Functions. XII, 582 pages. 2002.

Vol. 511: M. Külpmann, Stock Market Overreaction and Fundamental Valuation. IX, 198 pages. 2002.

Vol. 512: W.-B. Zhang, An Economic Theory of Cities.XI, 220 pages. 2002.

Vol. 513: K. Marti, Stochastic Optimization Techniques. VIII, 364 pages. 2002.

Vol. 514: S. Wang, Y. Xia, Portfolio and Asset Pricing. XII, 200 pages. 2002.

Vol. 515: G. Heisig, Planning Stability in Material Requirements Planning System. XII, 264 pages. 2002.

Vol. 516: B. Schmid, Pricing Credit Linked Financial Instruments. X, 246 pages. 2002.

Vol. 517: H. I. Meinhardt, Cooperative Decision Making in Common Pool Situations. VIII, 205 pages. 2002.

Vol. 518: S. Napel, Bilateral Bargaining. VIII, 188 pages. 2002.

Vol. 519: A. Klose, G. Speranza, L. N. Van Wassenhove (Eds.), Quantitative Approaches to Distribution Logistics and Supply Chain Management. XIII, 421 pages. 2002.

Vol. 520: B. Glaser, Efficiency versus Sustainability in Dynamic Decision Making. IX, 252 pages. 2002.

Vol. 521: R. Cowan, N. Jonard (Eds.), Heterogenous Agents, Interactions and Economic Performance. XIV, 339 pages. 2003.

Vol. 522: C. Neff, Corporate Finance, Innovation, and Strategic Competition. IX, 218 pages. 2003.

Vol. 523: W.-B. Zhang, A Theory of Interregional Dynamics. XI, 231 pages. 2003.

Vol. 524: M. Frölich, Programme Evaluation and Treatment Choise. VIII, 191 pages. 2003.

Vol. 525:S. Spinler, Capacity Reservation for Capital-Intensive Technologies. XVI, 139 pages. 2003.

Vol. 526: C. F. Daganzo, A Theory of Supply Chains. VIII, 123 pages. 2003.